CHAPTER 1

WHAT IS BIO FRIENDLY?

Our attitude towards gardening has changed in recent years. Nowadays we know that we must look after our plot with some thought for the environment. This calls for such measures as using natural products when we can and not using ozone-damaging ones.

Green gardening they call it. In the following pages you will find organic fertilizers and organic pesticides, but this book is not just about green gardening. The problem is that this concept covers only part of the safety needs of the living things in the garden.

Four biological groups meet in the plot at the back of the house. The first one, of course, is the living garden. The soil and plants .... and until the 1960s it was the only one we really cared about. Then we came to realise that we had a second biological group there — the animal population. This wildlife had to be cared for, and with the 1980s came the realisation that our garden was also a tiny part of a much larger biological group — the environment as a whole.

And that's where we stand today, Garden Friendly as ever and with a growing awareness that we must also be Animal Friendly and Environment Friendly. But there is also a fourth biological system in the garden and it does not have an active pressure group to campaign for its protection.

That fourth group consists of the people in the garden — you and the family. Every year about 400,000 accidents occur in the area around the house. About 250,000 need hospital treatment. This number is increasing, but merely going green is not the answer. These accidents are about falls and not fertilizers, about shocks and not sprays. So you must learn to be People Friendly .... for your own sake.

And that's what this book is about — the need to look after the garden, animals, environment .... and you.

GARDEN FRIENDLY
Improving the soil and caring for both the plants it supports and the non-living parts of the garden

Pages 2–49

ENVIRONMENT FRIENDLY
Avoiding harm wherever possible to the environment and the world's resources of materials in short supply

Pages 62–64

The Bio Friendly way to garden

ANIMAL FRIENDLY
Avoiding harm to pets and wildlife

Pages 59–61

PEOPLE FRIENDLY
Avoiding harm to you and your family

Pages 50–58

CHAPTER 2
Garden Friendly —
IMPROVING YOUR SOIL

It is quite stupid to regard your soil as a mere anchorage for your plants — something to be dug when the surface is hard, to be watered when dry and weeded when it looks untidy, but not to be tended like a living thing.

Soil *is* a living thing, with millions of micro-organisms and small creatures in a single handful. It is an unbelievably complex part of the natural system, and it is the main factor in determining whether you will succeed as a gardener.

The day you started to garden on that plot of soil you disturbed the delicate balance between the various elements. However green you try to be, gardening upsets the balance of Nature — a disturbing but inescapable fact. This means that the texture of the soil in bed, border or vegetable plot will be better or worse at this time next year. Which one depends on what you do before then.

Below is a plan to improve your soil. Follow it and you cannot fail to create a better crumb structure, an increase in the living population and better plant growth.

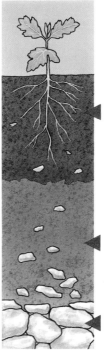

TOPSOIL is the fertile and living part of the soil. It is fertile because it contains nearly all of the humus, and it is living because it supports countless bacteria. These bacteria change various materials into plant foods. This layer varies from 2 in. in chalky soils to several feet in well-tended gardens. **When digging, this layer should be turned over, not buried under the subsoil.**

SUBSOIL lies under the topsoil. It can be recognised by its lighter colour, due to lack of humus. Soil structure is poor. **When digging, it should not be brought to the surface.**

BEDROCK is the mineral base below the subsoil. Usually it is the parent material of the soil above.

The [5 STEP] plan to improve your soil

Soil is composed of four basic components — minerals, organic matter, air and water. The physical quality of the blend is known as the soil texture or the soil structure — but these two terms do not mean the same thing.

SOIL TEXTURE refers to the proportions of different-sized mineral particles which are present in the soil. When coarse (sand) particles predominate the texture is *heavy*. When minute (clay) particles are plentiful the soil is described as *light*. **It is not practical to change the soil texture.**

SOIL STRUCTURE refers to the way the mineral particles are joined together in the soil. They may be almost unconnected as in a very light soil with little organic matter or they may be grouped in clods, plates or crumbs in a heavy soil. A crumb structure is the ideal — such soil is described as *friable*. **It is possible to change the soil structure** by following in order the steps set out below.

| STEP 1 | **Understand your soil.** Study the details of the various components shown on page 3 |

| STEP 2 | **Test your soil.** Before drawing up an improvement plan it is necessary to know whether the soil is light or heavy, acid or alkaline etc |

| STEP 3 | **Improve your soil by digging.** Don't make this an annual ritual on *all* bare land — it is not always necessary |

| STEP 4 | **Improve your soil by adding humus.** This step is *always* necessary, even in good soil |

| STEP 5 | **Improve your soil by adding calcium.** This step is necessary if the structure is poor |

STEP 1 · UNDERSTAND YOUR SOIL

MINERAL PARTICLES

The non-living skeleton of the soil which is derived from the decomposition of rocks by weathering. The fertility and size of these particles are governed by the type of parent rock.

Particle name is based on size. All **sands** have a gritty feel — **coarse sand** (0.6–2.0 mm in diameter) is distinctly gritty, **medium sand** (0.2–0.6 mm) feels like table salt and **fine sand** (0.02–0.2 mm) has a grittiness which is not easy to feel.

Silt (0.002–0.02 mm) has a silky or soapy feel. **Clay** (less than 0.002 mm) feels distinctly sticky.

AIR

Air is essential for the support of plant life and desirable soil life — it is also required for the steady breakdown of organic matter which releases nutrients. Movement of air is necessary to avoid the build-up of toxic gases — this air movement takes place through the soil pores.

HUMUS

Plant and animal remains are gradually decomposed in the soil. The agents of decay are the bacteria and other micro-scopic organisms. They break down dead roots and underground insects as well as fallen leaves carried below the soil surface by worms. Partially decomposed organic matter with the horde of living and dead bacteria is known as **humus** to the gardener. For the scientist it has a much narrower meaning. True humus is the dark, jelly-like substance which binds mineral particles into crumbs.

LIVING ORGANISMS

Millions of living organisms can be found in every ounce of soil. Most are microscopic — bacteria, fungi, eelworms etc. Others are small but visible — insects, seeds and so on. Worms and beetles are easily seen — the largest and least welcome living thing you are likely to find is the mole.

DEAD ORGANIC MATTER

The soil is the graveyard for roots, fallen leaves, insects etc as well as the organic materials (humus makers) we add to enrich it. Dead organic matter is *not* humus until it has decomposed. It does, however, serve as the base material for high bacterial activity and humus pro-duction. With this decomposition both major nutrients and trace elements are released into the soil. Some types of dead material may take many years to decompose.

STONES & GRAVEL

These are particles larger than 2 mm in diameter. 'Stones' usually refers to sizeable pieces of rock whereas 'gravel' usually describes the smaller weathered fragments — but there is no precise distinction.

WATER-BASED SOLUTION

This is often shortened to **soil water** but it is in fact a solution containing many dissolved inorganic and organic materials. Some (e.g nitrates, phosphates and potassium salts) are plant nutrients.

CRUMB

Crumbs range from lentil- to pea-sized. The spaces between them are known as **pores**.

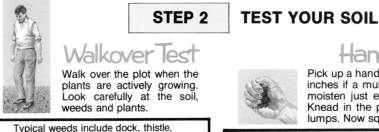

STEP 2   TEST YOUR SOIL

Walkover Test

Walk over the plot when the plants are actively growing. Look carefully at the soil, weeds and plants.

Typical weeds include dock, thistle, daisy and creeping buttercup. Rhododendron, Azalea and Camellia flourish with no foliage yellowing
ACID SOIL — See page 10

Typical weeds include clover and knapweed. Rhododendron, Azalea and Camellia show foliage yellowing
ALKALINE SOIL — See page 10

Rushes and sedges are present. The surface is covered with moss and/or green slime
POORLY-DRAINED SOIL — See page 10

Typical weeds include stinging nettle, sow-thistle, fat-hen, chickweed and groundsel
FERTILE SOIL

Pit Test

Dig a pit 2 ft x 2 ft x 2 ft during a period of dry weather. Look at the sides for a sub-surface pan — a hard layer with the texture and firmness of baked clay. Fill the pit with water — inspect after 24 hours.

Sub-surface pan present and/or water still present at the bottom of the pit
POORLY-DRAINED SOIL — See page 10

Near-black or grey topsoil — white subsoil a few inches below the surface
CHALKY SOIL — See column on right

Soil Kit Test

There are several kits available for testing the nitrogen, phosphates, potash and pH content of the soil. Some involve test-tubes and indicator solutions — others are based on a probe which is inserted into the ground. These kits provide a reasonably accurate way of discovering whether your soil needs liming or not (page 10), but are less useful and accurate for determining fertilizer needs (page 36).

Hand Test

Pick up a handful of soil — dig down a couple of inches if a mulch has been applied. If it is dry, moisten just enough to hold the soil together. Knead in the palm of the hand to break down lumps. Now squeeze the sample.

The soil forms a strong ball — when pressed it changes shape but does not fall apart. This ball feels smooth and sticky when wet

HEAVY (Clayey) SOIL

Good points: Generally well supplied with plant foods which are not leached away by rain. Good water retention.

Bad points: Difficult to work under most conditions. Cakes and cracks in dry weather — may waterlog in wet weather. Cold — not suitable for early crops.

Attend to drainage first if serious waterlogging is a problem — see page 10. Digging thoroughly in autumn will expose the clods to winter frosts — a generous quantity of organic matter should be incorporated at this time. Apply calcium in February to help crumb formation. Don't sow seed or plant out until the soil has sufficiently dried out in the spring. Mulch established plants.

The soil ball crumbles and sifts through the fingers. A small sample feels or sounds gritty when rubbed between finger and thumb. Does not stain the skin

LIGHT (Sandy) SOIL

Good points: Easy to work, even when wet. Free-draining in winter. Warm — suitable for early crops.

Bad points: Usually short of plant foods. Frequent watering is necessary in summer — shallow-rooted plants may die. Cools down rapidly at night and may cap badly.

Water and food shortage are constant problems, so incorporate plenty of organic matter into the top few inches in late winter or early spring. Digging may not be necessary — if it is then wait until early spring. Mulching is vital to conserve moisture and reduce leaching of plant nutrients — apply fertilizer in spring and summer.

The soil forms a distinct ball — when pressed it loses its shape and crumbles. It may feel slightly gritty — usually stains the skin

MEDIUM (Loamy) SOIL

Good points: Good crumb structure — possesses all the advantages, to a lesser degree, of both heavy and light soils.

Bad points: Surface capping takes place in wet weather if the silt content is high.

Try to keep it as it is, with regular dressings of humus-making materials and fertilizers. Occasional applications of calcium will be necessary — dig only if the soil is compacted.

The soil forms a distinct ball — when pressed it loses its shape and crumbles. The colour is black or greyish with white flecks. Check with pit test

CHALKY SOIL

Good points: Best soil type for some shrubs and many alpines. Usually free-draining and warm enough for early crops.

Bad points: Sticky and soft in wet weather — often parched in summer. Nutrients may be deficient — especially trace elements. Too alkaline for many plants.

Digging must be kept shallow — add plenty of humus-making materials. Use fertilizers and MultiTonic regularly. Green manuring (see page 7) is a great help — so is adding topsoil if the area is small. Although the bedrock is chalk, the soil is occasionally acid.

STEP 3 | IMPROVE YOUR SOIL BY DIGGING

Digging has a place in the soil improvement programme as it provides several benefits which are described below. But despite these benefits it is no longer regarded as an essential part of the programme to be carried out annually on every bit of bare land.

Digging incorporates manure or compost into the soil, buries annual weeds and exposes the roots of perennial ones. The basic purpose of digging, however, is to improve compacted soil by the direct action of the spade and the indirect action of frost and drying winds on the exposed clods. This means that it has an important role in breaking up land for the first time or breaking up heavy garden soil which has become caked on or below the surface.

It is not generally required on medium and light soils. Even in heavy soils it is worth considering building up raised beds (see page 29) rather than annual digging. The no-digging method involves the removal of weeds by surface cultivation with a rake or hoe and the application of a layer of bulky organic matter. This organic matter is taken into the soil by worms as well as by cultivation.

Continue annual digging by all means if you are fit and enjoy the exercise. Single digging (see below) is all you should need. Double digging is sometimes recommended for poorly-drained land — see The Garden Expert for details. Do be careful when digging. Dig at the wrong time and you can harm the soil — dig in the wrong way and you can harm yourself.

CHOOSE THE RIGHT TOOL: Use a spade for general work — make sure that it is not too heavy for you. Use a fork if the soil is very heavy or stony — a pickaxe may be required for breaking up a sub-surface pan or clay subsoil. Carry a scraper and use as necessary to keep the blade clean.

CHOOSE THE RIGHT SEASON: Very heavy soil should be dug before the end of November. Do not start too early — turning the soil over in September can produce a flush of weeds. Early winter is the best time for medium and heavy soils — wait until early spring before digging light land.

DIG AT THE RIGHT TIME: Never dig when the land is waterlogged or frozen. The soil should be dry enough not to stick to your footwear but wet enough to allow the blade to penetrate without a great deal of effort. Digging when the soil is too wet will damage rather than improve soil texture.

LEAVE THE SUBSOIL WHERE IT IS: Raw clay, chalk or sand brought to the surface will ruin the fertility of the soil.

DO NOT DISTURB THE DUG EARTH TOO QUICKLY: Leave the clods in lumps to ensure maximum benefit from the crumb-forming frosts of winter. Leave at least 3 weeks between digging and the preparation of the land for planting or seed sowing.

How to dig the safe way

(1) Wear clothes that will keep you warm — you should be neither hot nor cold when digging. Make sure your back is fully covered. Wear boots or stout shoes

(2) Try to keep your back straight — avoid any sudden twists from the hips and on no account strain harder than you are used to doing at home or at work

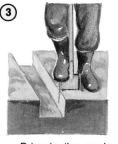

(3) Drive in the spade vertically to its full depth. Press (do not kick) down on the blade. This cut should be at right angles to the trench

(4) The next cut should be parallel to the trench, 6–8 in. behind the face. Do not be tempted to take larger slices

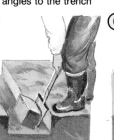

(5) Pull steadily (don't jerk) on the handle to lever the soil on to the blade

(6) Lift, and with a flick of the wrist turn the earth into the trench in front — turn the spadeful right over to bury the weeds

(7) Work for 10 minutes if you are out of condition — then lay down or do a non-strenuous job until you feel rested. Work for 20 minutes between rests if you are fit and used to physical exercise. For most people 30 minutes digging is quite enough for the first day

Dig out a trench about 10 in. wide and 1 spit deep. Move the soil to the other end of the plot. Spread compost or manure over the bottom of the trench — it is useful to incorporate Bone Meal at this stage.

Turn strip A into the trench. Annual weeds will be buried, but roots of perennial weeds (dandelions, nettles, docks etc) should be removed.

Work across the plot — a new trench will now have been created. Add Bone Meal, compost or manure as before and turn strip B into the trench. Continue with C etc. Use soil from the first trench to fill the final trench.

STEP 4	**IMPROVE YOUR SOIL BY ADDING HUMUS**

Soil bacteria hold the key to soil fertility. When alive they produce heat and transform complex organic materials into simple chemicals. When dead they release these plant-feeding materials plus colloidal gums. To the scientist it is these gums and not decomposing plant remains which are **humus** — the magical material which cements clay, silt and sand particles together to form soil crumbs.

Under natural conditions there is a rough balance which maintains the organic level of the soil. In a fertile soil there is a minimum of 5 per cent organic matter. Under cultivation this organic content decreases and the humus level falls. This means that you have to add **humus makers**. All are bulky organic materials which add to the humus content of the soil. When in addition these materials release plant nutrients they can be called **manures**. This means that garden compost and seaweed are manures and peat is not.

Types of Humus Maker

RAW HUMUS MAKERS
Examples: Grass clippings, fresh dung, dug-in weeds. These organic materials contain sufficient nutrients to stimulate bacterial growth. Heat is produced and soil structure is improved.

Using raw humus makers is a good way of warming the earth and raising its humus content — provided you allow for the drawbacks. The rapid build-up of bacteria robs the soil of nitrogen — always add a nitrogen-rich fertilizer. Heat is generated — use some time before planting and keep it well away from roots.

MATURED HUMUS MAKERS
Examples: Well-rotted manure or compost, Bio Friendly Humus. These organic materials do not contain sufficient nutrients to stimulate bacterial growth. They have been produced from raw humus makers by composting.

The warming effect is lost but this is outweighed by the advantages. Tender roots are not damaged and the nitrogen in the soil is not locked up. Unlike the types described below these materials have more than a simple opening-up effect. The humus which was produced during the composting process promotes crumb formation when they are added to the soil.

FIBROUS MATERIALS
Examples: Peat, bark, sawdust. These organic materials are rich in cellulose but lack sugars and starches. There is little or no bacterial activity and so they are ineffective humus makers. Peat acts as a sponge, improving air- and water-holding capacity. Conservationists worry about its wholesale use as a general soil treatment, as supplies are limited — see page 62. Peat decomposes slowly or hardly at all, but sawdust and some bark products break down more quickly. Add a nitrogen-rich fertilizer when using sawdust.

You don't have to choose between HUMUS MAKERS and FERTILIZERS — both are essential

There is a great deal of confusion about the roles and relative merits of humus makers (animal manure, straw, well-rotted garden compost etc) and fertilizers (dried blood, bone meal etc). The truth of the matter is that both groups have their own special job to do — and there is not much overlap.

HUMUS MAKERS are bulky organic materials — a typical application rate is a bucketful per sq. yard. They are added to the soil to add fibre and/or to build up the bacterial population. In this way **they improve the structure of the soil.**

Nutrients are usually present, but only in the case of top-quality animal manure applied at a high rate is the supply adequate. The plant food content is usually low, slow-acting and wrongly balanced. Fertilizers have to be used to get the full benefit from humus makers.

FERTILIZERS are materials containing one or more major plant nutrients in concentrated form — a typical application rate is a handful per sq. yard. These powders, granules or liquids are added to the soil where **they feed the plants.**

These dressings cannot be expected to make any significant contribution to the humus content of the soil, even when they are organic-based and are claimed to improve the soil. Humus makers have to be used to get the full benefit from fertilizers. See page 37 for a list of organic and natural plant foods.

Humus maker	Nitrogen % N	Phosphates % P$_2$O$_5$	Potash % K$_2$O	Application rate	Notes
BARK	¼	*	*	1 in. layer over soil surface — dig in or use as a surface mulch	Bark chippings (pulverised, shredded, granular etc) are now offered as a peat substitute. Very useful for mulching (see page 9) because bark is a dense material, but less useful for digging in
BIO FRIENDLY HUMUS	½	*	*	¼ lb per yd of seed drill before sowing or ¼ lb–2 lb under roots before planting	See page 32 for details
COMPOST	1½	2	½	1 bucket per sq. yd — dig in or use as a surface mulch	See page 8 for details
FARMYARD MANURE	½	¼	½	1 bucket per sq. yd — dig in or use as a surface mulch	Before use, stack it under some form of roofing, cover with several inches of soil and leave to decay. It is ready when the smell has disappeared and the straw is no longer recognisable
GREEN MANURE	2	¼	¾	Dig in during summer/autumn	Green manure is a crop grown for digging in and providing humus for chalky or sandy soil. Apply a fertilizer and sow rape or mustard in April–July. Dig in 2 months after germination
LEAFMOULD	½	¼	¼	1 bucket per sq. yd — dig in or use as a surface mulch	Collect leaves in autumn (Oak and Beech are the favourites) and build a heap — 6 in. layers of leaves between 1 in. layers of soil. Composting is slow — leave for a year
MUSHROOM COMPOST	½	¼	½	1 bucket per sq. yd — dig in before planting	Used to be stable manure plus soil, straw and chalk — nowadays it is composted straw. A useful material for enriching sandy soil. Do not use if you intend to grow lime haters
PEAT	¾	*	*	Use in planting mixture or as a surface mulch	There are two types. Sedge peat is a little richer in nitrogen and breaks down more quickly in the soil. Sphagnum peat holds more air and water — use when planting lime haters
POULTRY MANURE	2	1½	1	Compost before use	Fresh poultry manure is rich in nutrients — unfortunately it is also rich in materials which can be toxic to young roots. The best plan is to add poultry manure to the compost heap
SAWDUST	¼	*	*	Compost before use or apply 1 in. layer over soil surface	Cheap, but use with care. It will rob the soil of nitrogen, so add 1 oz of nitrogen per cubic ft of sawdust before digging into the soil. Another problem is that it may contain toxic resins
SEAWEED	¼	¼	½	1 bucket per sq. yd — dig in before planting	An excellent manure maker — free for the taking if you live near the sea. Dig in without composting — both the humus and trace element content of the soil will be enriched. Wash off the salt before use
SEWAGE SLUDGE (DRIED)	5	4	2	2–3 lb per sq. yd — dig in during autumn/winter	Never use raw sewage — buy activated sludge. Wear gloves when applying. Not much organic matter is applied per sq. yd but it is a fairly effective source of plant nutrients
STABLE MANURE	¾	¼	½	1 bucket per sq. yd — dig in or use as a surface mulch	Best type of manure for heavy soils. Should contain plenty of straw. Do not use it immediately. Stack it under cover for several months — see farmyard manure above
STRAW	½	*	¾	Compost before use	Straw is an active humus maker when plenty of nitrogen is present, but it is not a good idea to add it directly to the soil. It often contains weedkillers, and so it should be composted before use

* = less than ¼ %

Compost Making | a key feature in the Bio Friendly garden

Much of this chapter on soil improvement is devoted to one simple fact — you have to add a large amount of organic matter to your plot every year. Relying solely on shop-bought material is far too expensive a proposition — you have to learn to make compost. More nonsense has been written about compost making than any other gardening subject. We still read about helpful lime, harmful soil, the need to turn and the value of a nitrogen-rich activator. All these things are quite wrong if your starting point is mainly grass clippings, which is exactly the situation in most gardens.

THE PROBLEM

Successful composting takes place only when there is intense bacterial and fungal activity. Heat is generated and humus is formed. For this to take place you need starting material with 30 parts of carbon to 1 part of nitrogen.

A mixture of grass, straw and chopped up fibrous stems could well have this ratio, but a mixture of grass clippings, green weeds and a few prunings contains too much nitrogen for active bacterial growth. A *nitrogen* additive could make matters worse — what you need is a *carbon-rich* additive and a revolutionary technique — the Recycling Method.

THE ANSWER
— the Recycling Method

The Recycling Method turns the Traditional Method on its head. Lime is left out but a sprinkling of soil is added. Turning is prohibited and a waterproof cover is absolutely vital. Water is never added.

This may all sound revolutionary, but the technique was thoroughly tested with 200 Horticultural Societies in 1980. More than 90% found that the Recycling Method gave better results than the Traditional Method when used with lawn mowings alone or with a mixture of greenstuff.

THE GOOD CONTAINER

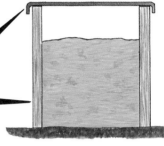

LARGE
One big one always beats 2 small ones

WATERPROOF COVER
Rain must be kept out of the heap. Use a rigid cover or a sheet of plastic

THICK WALLS
Wood, breeze blocks, solid plastic and bricks are all suitable. Keeping the heat in is one of the secrets of making good compost

... AND THE BAD

SMALL
Contents cool down too quickly

OPEN TOP
Rainwater stops bacterial activity — secondary fermentation turns the compost into green, smelly sludge

THIN PLASTIC OR WIRE NETTING
Vital heat is lost — it is this heat which kills weed seeds and breaks down organic matter. Put boards or bags round the sides if you can or lean it against a wall — line wire bins or plastic bags with old newspapers

The simple 5 step technique

Most sorts of container will do — the best ones have sides to keep the heat in. A cover to keep the rain out is vital.

1. **Make a layer of greenstuff** about 9 in. deep. This layer should be flat, not heaped in the middle.
2. **Sprinkle a thin layer of Bio Friendly Compost Maker** over the surface. This contains bacterial stimulants in a carbon-rich base and is 100% organic. A large handful should cover about 1 sq. yard.
3. **Cover with a thin layer of soil** to provide bacteria, mop up undesirable gases and absorb water.
4. **Continue in this way** until all the greenstuff is used.
5. **Cover the top** to keep out the rain.

Next time you mow or have waste greenstuff simply repeat the process on top of the previous pile. Never let air into the centre of the compost by turning or making holes in the heap.

If the waste material is mainly strawy or woody rather than soft and green, you need to use a nitrogen-rich activator rather than Bio Friendly Compost Maker. Bio Friendly Plant Food or Dried Blood can be used for this purpose.

WHAT GOES IN

Use lawn mowings, vegetable and flower stalks, leaves, annual weeds, peat, soft hedge clippings, bracken, straw, smashed-up brassica stalks, tea leaves, peelings, household vegetable waste and egg shells. The lawn weedkiller in grass mowings will break down in 6–9 months if the technique described above is carried out. Test before using — see right. Do *not* use twigs, roots of perennial weeds, badly diseased plants or meat and fish waste from the kitchen. If you have to burn non-compostable woody material do read the section on bonfires (page 58) first.

... AND WHAT COMES OUT

The compost is ready when it is crumbly and there is no unpleasant smell. It will be brown rather than green and individual ingredients will not be recognisable. A heap made in the spring or summer should be ready in late autumn or the following spring. Autumn compost should be used for digging in — spring material is excellent for mulching. It is wise to test compost made with clippings from a weedkiller-treated lawn. Mix a sample with some peat-based compost and sow Cress or Radish seed — normal germination means that the garden compost can be used.

Mulching | a key feature in the Bio Friendly garden

Mulching really comes into its own in Bio Friendly gardening. The need to build up the humus content of the soil is vital, and the need to suppress weeds around plants without resorting to modern weedkillers makes mulching a must. Yet most gardeners do not mulch at all, and those who do generally misunderstand and underuse the technique. Basically a mulch is a layer of material placed around plants in order to improve the soil and plant growth and/or to suppress weed growth. On this page you will learn why, where, how and when to mulch.

THE HUMUS MULCH

Humus mulches are bulky organic materials which improve the soil, stimulate plant growth and suppress annual weeds. Use one of the following:

- **Moist peat**
- **Shredded bark**
- **Leaf mould**
- **Garden compost**
- **Well-rotted manure**
- **Mushroom compost**
- **Bio Friendly Humus**
- **Straw + nitrogen fertilizer**
- **Grass clippings** — thin layer only, must be weedkiller free
- **Contents of used growing bags**

WHAT THE MULCH DOES

The soil below is kept moist in summer, reducing the need to water. It is also kept cool, and research has shown that this moist and cool root zone promotes more active growth than in unmulched areas
•
The soil is kept warmer than uncovered ground in winter — a definite benefit for many plants
•
Soil structure is improved for a number of reasons. Humus is added, earthworm activity is increased and surface capping is eliminated
•
Annual weed growth is suppressed — those which break through are easily removed by hand pulling so there is no need to hoe. Vigorous perennial weeds will come through — consider a weed control mulch if these are a problem
•
Some pests and diseases are kept in check. Obviously root flies are deterred and so are moles. U.S research has shown that eelworms are kept in check
•
Vegetables are protected from rain splashes bouncing off the soil — a much ignored problem
•
Humus mulches are insulators which retain the conditions occurring at the time they are put down. So the soil at this time should be just right — warm and moist and never cold and dry

Where to mulch

There are two basic areas:

UNCULTIVATED GROUND The weed control problem can be a headache, especially if the soil is fertile. Try mulching as an alternative to digging or herbicide treatment. Use a weed control mulch — cut slits and use as planting holes. Make sure that holes or slits are present in plastic sheeting to allow entry of rainwater to the soil beneath.

AROUND GROWING PLANTS Humus mulches and weed control mulches covered with organic material are placed around ornamental shrubs and trees, herbaceous border plants and on the vegetable plot.

How & when to mulch

The standard time for applying a humus mulch is May. Success largely depends on preparing the soil surface properly before adding the organic blanket. Remove debris, dead leaves and weeds, and then water the surface if it is dry. Apply a spring feed if this has not been done and hoe in lightly. It is essential that the soil should be reasonably warm before a mulch is applied — delay the operation if there is a cold snap.

The soil is moist and warm — spread a 2–3 inch layer over the area which is under the branches and leaves. Do not take the mulch right up to the stems — a build-up of moist organic material can lead to rotting. Do not disturb this layer during the summer months, but in October it should be hoed or lightly forked into the top inch of soil.

Some people wait until early spring so that frost will be prevented from getting down to the roots, but a mulch in early spring will increase the risk of air frost around the plants. Move the mulch in October or mid March — either way the ground should be bare until it has warmed up in May. At this time the mulch should be renewed.

Black polythene sheeting can be used as a weed control mulch in the vegetable garden or allotment. Strips of plastic are laid across the prepared soil in March and the edges buried under the surface. Slits are cut in the surface to act as planting holes, and growth is stimulated by the moist conditions below. Potatoes do not need earthing up and Strawberries, Marrows and Courgettes are kept off the ground.

THE WEED CONTROL MULCH

Weed control mulches are forms of organic or inorganic sheeting which suppress perennial as well as annual weeds. Improvement to soil structure is either slight or does not take place. Weed control mulches are often covered with shredded bark, peat, earth etc where appearance is important. Use one of the following:

- **Polythene sheeting** — 150 gauge will last for one season
- **Cardboard** — use old boxes
- **Woven plastic** — keeps weeds down but lets water through. Several proprietary brands available e.g Ground Cover
- **Carpeting**
- **Newspaper** — use several sheets

STEP 5 — IMPROVE YOUR SOIL BY ADDING CALCIUM

Calcium has a vital role to play in the soil. It is one of the essential elements for all plants, but its most dramatic effect is on heavy soils. The tiny particles of clay group together in the presence of calcium to form crumbs — this process known as flocculation leads to an improvement in structure.

This improvement, however, is short lived and these flocculated crumbs must be 'fixed' by humus or the effect is lost. Rain steadily washes lime out of the soil at an average rate of ½ oz per sq. yard each year. Slowly the land becomes more acid, and neither humus makers nor the majority of fertilizers are of any help. You have to use either lime or gypsum — which one depends on the acidity of the soil and the plants you grow.

Which one to use

SOURCE OF CALCIUM	BENEFITS
LIME (calcium hydroxide or calcium carbonate) This calcium source reduces acidity	**NEUTRALISES ACIDITY** Very few plants grow well in acid soil and Bacteria and earthworms decline in acid soil
Various forms are available. **Chalk** and **ground limestone** are slow-acting. **Dolomite limestone** contains magnesium — this is the recommended type. **Calcified seaweed** (coral) is the 'organic' form — long-lasting and expensive. **Hydrated lime** (slaked lime) is by far the most popular type. It is cheaper, stronger and quicker-acting than the others	**IMPROVES STRUCTURE OF HEAVY SOIL** Calcium binds clay particles into soil crumbs
	SERVES AS ONE OF THE PLANT FOODS Calcium is needed in moderate amounts by plants
Do test your soil before liming — see page 4. If an excessive amount is used, humus breaks down too quickly and some plant leaves turn yellow because of the lock-up of iron and manganese	**FREES NUTRIENTS** Elements locked up by clay particles are freed
	DISCOURAGES SOME SOIL PESTS Examples include club root, slugs and wireworms

SOURCE OF CALCIUM
GYPSUM (calcium sulphate) This calcium source *does not* reduce acidity
Sold under various trade names — sometimes used as a gypsum/ dolomite limestone mixture
It is used where heavy soil is not acid, or where the soil is acid but is used for lime-hating plants such as Rhododendron

POORLY-DRAINED SOIL

Poor drainage is a plant killer. Roots are starved of air, rotting organisms abound and toxic gases build up. This condition is usually associated with heavy topsoil — improve the structure by cultural means. Impeded drainage is a much more serious problem — downward movement of water is blocked and not just slowed down. There are 3 prime causes — non-porous rock close to the surface, a sub-surface pan (see page 4) or a high water table in a wetland area. Whatever the cause, it will be necessary to do something.

● Create a crumb structure in heavy soil. Study this chapter carefully — dig, add as much humus maker as you can and then add calcium.

● Break through the sub-surface pan if one is present. Use a garden fork or pickaxe as appropriate.

● If the cause is non-porous rock or a high water table, you have a serious problem. Laying drains or building a soakaway is usually impractical — the easiest way is to add topsoil and/or create raised beds (page 29).

How much to use

Your garden can have too much of a good thing. If an excessive amount of lime is used, humus breaks down too quickly and plant leaves turn yellow. It is easy to avoid overliming by testing your soil and applying the rate recommended below.

	Hydrated Lime application rate*		
	Light soil	**Medium soil**	**Heavy soil**
VERY ACID	1 lb per sq. yd	1½ lb per sq. yd	2 lb per sq. yd
ACID	½ lb per sq. yd	1 lb per sq. yd	1½ lb per sq. yd
NEARLY NEUTRAL	¼ lb per sq. yd	½ lb per sq. yd	1 lb per sq. yd
ALKALINE	do not lime	do not lime	do not lime
NOT TESTED	½ lb per sq. yd	½ lb per sq. yd	¾ lb per sq. yd

* with limestone increase rates by 25%

Gypsum application rate
½ lb per sq. yd

When to apply

The best time to add lime is after digging in autumn. If autumn manuring has been carried out, postpone liming until February. Spread evenly over the surface.

Vegetable plot: Lime every 3 years. If you follow a crop rotation, lime the plot which is intended for the Cabbage family. Do not lime land to be used for Potatoes.

Flower garden: Lime every 2 years on light soils, and every 3 years on medium and heavy soils.

Do not mix it with other soil dressings. To avoid the loss of plant foods, lime should not be applied until at least 2–3 months after manuring, and 1 month after fertilizers. Compost, fertilizers and seeds can safely be applied 1 month after liming.

The best time to add gypsum to the soil is in the autumn. Repeat the treatment in the spring if the soil structure is very poor.

CHAPTER 3
Garden Friendly —
GROWING THE PLANTS

ROSES
Deciduous Shrubs and Trees of the genus Rosa, usually listed separately in the catalogues because of their importance and great popularity

A **Half Standard** is a Rose Tree with a 2½ ft stem

A **Full Standard** is a Rose Tree with a 3½ ft stem

WOODY PLANTS
Perennial plants with woody stems which survive the winter

A **Tree** bears only one woody stem at ground level

A **Shrub** bears several woody stems at ground level

A **Climber** has the ability when established to attach itself to or twine around an upright structure. Some weak-stemmed plants which require tying to stakes (e.g Climbing Roses) are included here

A **Hedge** is a continuous line of Shrubs or Trees in which the individuality of each plant is partly or wholly lost

EVERGREEN SHRUBS & TREES
Woody plants which retain their leaves during winter

Conifers bear cones and nearly all are Evergreens

Semi-evergreens (e.g Privet) retain most of their leaves in a mild winter

DECIDUOUS SHRUBS & TREES
Woody plants which shed their leaves in winter

Tree Fruit are Trees which produce edible fruit (e.g Apple, Pear, Peach, Plum)

Soft Fruit are Shrubs and Climbers which produce edible fruit (e.g Blackcurrant, Gooseberry). A few are Herbaceous Plants (e.g Strawberry)

A **Ground Cover** is a low-growing and spreading plant which forms a dense, leafy mat

TURF PLANTS
Low-growing carpeting plants, nearly always members of the Grass Family, which can be regularly mown and walked upon

VEGETABLES
Plants which are grown for their edible roots, stems or leaves. A few are grown for their fruits (e.g Tomato, Cucumber, Marrow, Capsicum)

HERBS
Plants which are grown for their medicinal value, their culinary value as garnishes or flavourings, or their cosmetic value as sweet-smelling flowers or leaves

HERBACEOUS PLANTS
Plants with non-woody stems which generally die down in winter

BULBS
Bulbs (more correctly Bulbous Plants) produce underground fleshy organs which are offered for sale for planting indoors or outdoors. Included here are the **True Bulbs, Corms, Rhizomes** and **Tubers**

BIENNIALS
Plants which complete their life span, from seed to death, in two seasons

A **Hardy Biennial** (HB) is sown outdoors in summer, producing stems and leaves in the first season and flowering in the next

Some Perennials are treated as Biennials (e.g Wallflower, Daisy)

PERENNIALS
Plants which complete their life span, from seed to death, in three or more seasons

A **Hardy Perennial** (HP) will live for years in the garden — the basic plant of the herbaceous border

A **Half-hardy Perennial** (HHP) is not fully hardy and needs to spend its winter in a frost-free place (e.g Fuchsia, Geranium)

A **Greenhouse Perennial** (GP) is not suitable for outdoor cultivation

A **Rockery Perennial** (RP) is a dwarf Hardy Perennial suitable for growing in a rockery. **Alpine** is an alternative name, although some originated on the shore rather than on mountains, and some delicate True Alpines need to be grown indoors

ANNUALS
Plants which complete their life span, from seed to death, in a single season

A **Hardy Annual** (HA) is sown outdoors in spring

A **Half-hardy Annual** (HHA) cannot withstand frost, and so it is raised under glass and planted outdoors when the danger of frost is past

A **Greenhouse** (or **Tender**) **Annual** (GA) is too susceptible to cold weather for outdoor cultivation, but may be planted out for a short time in summer

A **Bedding Plant** is an Annual, Biennial or occasionally a Perennial set out in quantity in autumn or spring to provide a temporary display

THE BIO FRIENDLY WAY TO CARE FOR *Lawns*

It is sad to hear the view that a lawn is not an essential feature of the organic garden. If your plot is very small or heavily shaded then it might be impractical to have one. For the rest it *is* an essential feature — a place for you to sit and a place for children to play.

Begin properly. Read the detailed instructions set out in The Lawn Expert. Sowing seed is the cheapest method, but for most people the hard work and expense of turfing is worthwhile in order to have a mature-looking lawn in a matter of weeks.

The maintenance programme depends on what you want. For the showpiece lawn there is top-dressing every autumn, spiking at regular intervals, brushing before every cut and so on. But maintaining a standard utility lawn is much simpler — just follow the plan below.

Mow regularly

The most important step of all. Buy a mower with sufficient power for the area involved. Make sure the blades are sharp and properly set. Begin in March and finish in October. Mowing is required once a week in spring and autumn and in times of drought, twice a week when the grass is growing actively in summer. The recommended height is ½ in. for a fine luxury lawn and 1 in. for a standard utility one. Read the 'lawn mowers' section on page 54 to avoid accidents.

Put on a spring dressing

Cutting regularly takes a lot of food out of the soil, and an impoverished lawn invites weed and moss invasion. A late spring dressing is essential and you have a choice of two. Lawn Sand is the age-old remedy for pale grass, weeds and moss. Do not overdose — use Velvas which has a blue colour to show you where you've been. Water in thoroughly 2 days after treatment. If there are few weeds and no moss, use non-scorching Bio Lawn Tonic instead.

Trim the edges

A lawn with overgrown grass at the edges can be an eyesore. Make sure the mower can reach right up to the edge — then trim around the edges after mowing. There are many varieties of equipment for this job.

Rake during the spring and again in the autumn

Raking with a spring-tine rake has several benefits. The build-up of dead thatch is prevented and surface debris is removed. The clearing away of fallen leaves in autumn is essential — never leave them on the surface over winter.

Water *before* the grass turns brown

The first effect of drought on lawns is a loss of springiness and a general dullness of the turf. Look for these signs after about 7–10 days of dry weather. If seen then water copiously — a light sprinkling every few days can do more harm than good. You should put on enough water to go down 4 in. — this will be about 3 gallons per sq. yard. Water every 4–10 days.

Don't let weeds get out of hand

Weeds spotted here and there on the lawn can be dug out with a small trowel and the holes filled with compost or peat. If there are deep roots you can dab the leaves with a spot weedkiller such as the Bio Weed Pencil — do read the precautions and wash your hands after use. If the weed problem is widespread and includes creeping sorts then Lawn Sand (see above) is the answer.

THE BIO FRIENDLY WAY TO GROW

Each year the members of the Royal National Rose Society vote on the best and most popular Roses — the result of the latest poll is listed below. If your search is for reliability rather than novelty, this Rose Analysis is an excellent guide.

HYBRID TEA ROSES
new name:
LARGE-FLOWERED ROSES

The most popular class. The flower stems are long and the blooms are shapely. The typical Hybrid Tea has medium-sized or large blooms with many petals forming a distinct cone.

Position	Name	Colour	Height (ft)	Petals
1	SILVER JUBILEE	Peach pink & cream	2½	25
2	PEACE	Yellow, flushed pink	4½	45
3	JUST JOEY	Coppery pink & buff	2½	30
4	WENDY CUSSONS	Rose red	3¼	35
5=	ALEXANDER	Bright vermilion	5	25
5=	FRAGRANT CLOUD	Coral red	3	30
7	ALEC'S RED	Light crimson	3	45
8	ERNEST H. MORSE	Rich red	3	30
9	GRANDPA DICKSON	Lemon yellow	2¾	35
10	BLESSINGS	Rose pink touched salmon	3	30
11	PICCADILLY	Scarlet; yellow reverse	2½	25
12=	SUPER STAR	Vermilion	3¼	35
12=	WHISKY MAC	Amber yellow	2½	30
14	ROSE GAUJARD	Carmine & white	3½	30
15	TROIKA	Orange-bronze, flushed red	3	30
16	PASCALI	White; pale buff base	3¼	25
17=	MISCHIEF	Coral salmon	2¾	30
17=	PRIMA BALLERINA	Deep rose pink	2½	25

FLORIBUNDA ROSES
new name:
CLUSTER-FLOWERED ROSES

The Floribunda bears its flowers in clusters or trusses, and several blooms in each one open at the same time. In general the flower form is inferior to a Hybrid Tea.

Position	Name	Colour	Height (ft)	Petals
1	ICEBERG	White	4	25
2	QUEEN ELIZABETH	Pink	5	30
3	MARGARET MERRIL	Pearly white	3	25
4	KORRESIA	Bright yellow	2½	35
5=	AMBER QUEEN	Orange-buff	2	40
5=	EVELYN FISON	Bright scarlet	2½	30
7	MOUNTBATTEN	Mimosa yellow	4¼	45
8	ELIZABETH OF GLAMIS	Orange-salmon	3	35
9	ALLGOLD	Bright yellow	2	20
10	SOUTHAMPTON	Apricot orange, flushed red	3½	25
11=	GLENFIDDICH	Golden amber	2¾	25
11=	MATANGI	Vermilion; white eye	2¾	25
13=	ARTHUR BELL	Bright yellow	3¼	20
13=	ANNE HARKNESS	Apricot yellow	5	25
15=	DEAREST	Salmon pink	2½	30
15=	MASQUERADE	Yellow & red	3½	15
17	ENGLISH MISS	Light rose pink	2½	35
18	CITY OF LEEDS	Salmon pink	2½	25

There is one snag to growing Roses organically. You will have no problem feeding them and you should be able to keep the major pests under control with organic sprays. The snag is disease control if you do not wish to use a modern systemic fungicide — the natural ones are less effective than complex chemical treatments against the major diseases.

The first thing you must do is to pick your new Roses with care. Check that they have good disease resistance — a copy of The Rose Expert will be helpful. Next, you must pay extra attention to all cultural rules so as to cut down the risk of disease infection.

Prepare the soil thoroughly before planting — dig in a good supply of organic matter plus a dressing of a fertilizer such as Bio Friendly Plant Food. Let the soil settle for at least 6 weeks before planting. If the soil is not ideal put a 1 in. layer of peat or Bio Friendly Humus into the planting hole and stir into the soil. Don't plant Roses under trees and make sure that there will be plenty of fresh air around the bushes. Choose a sunny spot.

With established Roses prune in early spring. Don't force your secateurs to cut through branches more than ½ in. across — use a saw. Give the plants a spring dressing of Bio Friendly Plant Food and put down a humus mulch in May — see page 9. An added benefit here is the prevention of disease spores being splashed up from the soil by raindrops. Apply a second fertilizer dressing in June or July.

Make sure the bushes do not go short of water — dryness at the roots stimulates mildew. Keep watch for aphids — if they are clustered on young growth then use a Bio Friendly Pest Pistol (horticultural soap). Pick off caterpillars and rolled leaves — dead-head faded blooms to ensure a regular succession of flowering shoots.

Use Bio Friendly Pest & Disease Duster when the first spots of mildew appear — don't let it get out of hand on a disease-prone variety. Black spot can be more of a problem, especially if you live in a pure air district. Pick off diseased leaves — remove all fallen leaves in winter.

Rose rust is the major headache — coloured pustules appear on the underside of leaves. Once rare but now spreading, this disease seriously damages the plant and is often fatal. If it takes hold you will have to spray with Systhane — see page 47.

THE BIO FRIENDLY WAY TO GROW

Bedding Plants

Viola hybrida 'Blue Heaven'

Bedding plants are annuals plus some biennials and perennials which are set out in quantity to provide a temporary display. Planting takes place in spring for a summer display and in autumn for a spring showing. Many of the popular summer bedding plants are half-hardy annuals — make sure that the seedlings are properly hardened off and don't put them out whilst the risk of frost remains.

People can't agree whether spring bulbs should be included in this group — some books do but garden centres don't. In this book the group is restricted to plants which are green and growing at the time of transplanting.

Buy in containers such as small pots or seed trays — avoid if you can a few plants with roots wrapped in newspaper. Lift out of trays by gently prising up with a trowel and placing in the planting hole in one operation —don't lift a clump and leave it beside you to dry out. The soil should not be too rich — never overfeed. Water to keep the soil moist until the plants are established and lift out any mouldy plants as soon as they are seen.

Dahlia 'Coltness Gem'

Latin name	Common name	Site & soil	Type	Spacing	Flowering period	Height
ABUTILON	Abutilon	Sunny site — well-drained soil	HHP	Dot plant	Dappled foliage — not grown for flowers	3–4 ft
AGERATUM	Floss Flower	Sun or light shade — ordinary soil	HHA	8 in.	June–October	8 in.
ALYSSUM	Sweet Alyssum	Sunny site — well-drained soil	HA	9 in.	June–September	3–6 in.
AMARANTHUS	Love-lies-bleeding	Sunny site — well-drained soil	HHA	Dot plant	July–October	3 ft
ANTIRRHINUM	Snapdragon	Sunny site — well-drained soil	HHA	9 in.–1½ ft	July–October	6 in.–4 ft
BEGONIA	Bedding Begonia	Partial shade — humus-rich soil	HHA	5–15 in.	June–September	6 in.–1½ ft
BELLIS	Double Daisy	Sun or light shade — ordinary soil	HB	6 in.	March–July	3–6 in.
CALCEOLARIA	Slipper Flower	Sunny site — ordinary soil	HHA	9 in.	June–October	1 ft
CALLISTEPHUS	China Aster	Sunny site — well-drained soil	HHA	9 in.–1½ ft	August–October	9 in.–2½ ft
CAMPANULA	Canterbury Bell	Sunny site — well-drained soil	HB	1 ft	May–July	1½–2½ ft
CANNA	Indian Shot	Sunny site — humus-rich soil	HHP	Dot plant	August–October	3–4 ft
CELOSIA	Celosia	Sunny site — avoid heavy soil	HHA	9 in.–1 ft	July–September	9 in.–2 ft
CHEIRANTHUS	Wallflower	Sunny site — non-acid soil	HB	8 in.–1 ft	March-May	9 in.–2 ft
CHRYSANTHEMUM	Annual Chrysanthemum	Sunny site — non-acid soil	HA	1 ft	July–September	1½–2 ft
COLEUS	Flame Nettle	Sun or light shade — ordinary soil	HHA	1 ft	Coloured foliage — not grown for flowers	1 ft
DAHLIA	Bedding Dahlia	Sunny site — avoid light soil	HHA	1 ft	July–November	1–2 ft

HA = *hardy annual*   HHA = *half-hardy annual*   HB = *hardy biennial*   HHP = *half-hardy perennial*
Dot plant = *tall specimen plant with showy leaves and/or flowers*

Latin name	Common name	Site & soil	Type	Spacing	Flowering period	Height
DATURA	Angel's Trumpet	Sunny site — humus-rich soil	HHP	Dot plant	August–October	4–6 ft
DIANTHUS	Sweet William	Sunny site — non-acid soil	HB	9 in.	June–July	1–2 ft
FUCHSIA	Fuchsia	Sun or light shade — ordinary soil	HHP	1–2½ ft	July–October	1–4 ft
HELIOTROPIUM	Heliotrope	Sunny site — well-drained soil	HHA	1 ft	June–September	1½ ft
IBERIS	Candytuft	Sunny site — well-drained soil	HA	9 in.	May–August	9 in.–1½ ft
IMPATIENS	Busy Lizzie	Sun or shade — well-drained soil	HHA	6–9 in.	June–October	6 in.–1 ft
KOCHIA	Burning Bush	Sun or light shade — ordinary soil	HHA	1½–2 ft	Red autumn foliage — not grown for flowers	2 ft
LOBELIA	Lobelia	Sun or light shade — ordinary soil	HHA	6 in.	June–September	4–8 in.
MATTHIOLA	Brompton Stock	Sun or light shade — well-drained soil	HB	9 in.–1 ft	March–May	1–2 ft
MATTHIOLA	Ten Week Stock	Sun or light shade — well-drained soil	HHA	9 in.–1 ft	June–August	1–2½ ft
MESEMBRYANTHEMUM	Livingstone Daisy	Sunny site — well-drained soil	HHA	8 in.	July–September	4–6 in.
MIMULUS	Monkey Flower	Partial shade — moist soil	HHA	9 in.	June–September	9 in.
MYOSOTIS	Forget-me-not	Light shade — well-drained soil	HB	8 in.	April–May	6 in.–1 ft
NEMESIA	Nemesia	Sun or light shade — ordinary soil	HHA	6 in.	June–September	9 in.–1½ ft
NICOTIANA	Tobacco Plant	Sun or light shade — well-drained soil	HHA	9 in.–1 ft	June–October	9 in.–3 ft
PELARGONIUM	Geranium	Sun or light shade — well-drained soil	HHP	1 ft	July–October	1–2 ft
PETUNIA	Petunia	Sunny site — ordinary soil	HHA	6 in.–1 ft	June–October	6 in.–1½ ft
PHLOX	Annual Phlox	Sunny site — well-drained soil	HHA	8 in.	June–September	6 in.–1½ ft
PRIMULA	Polyanthus	Partial shade — moist soil	HB	1 ft	March–May	1 ft
RICINUS	Castor-oil Plant	Sun or light shade — ordinary soil	HHA	Dot plant	Large foliage — not grown for flowers	5 ft
SALVIA	Scarlet Sage	Sunny site — ordinary soil	HHA	1 ft	June–October	9 in.–1½ ft
SCABIOSA	Sweet Scabious	Sunny site — well-drained soil	HA	1 ft	July–October	1½ ft
SCHIZANTHUS	Poor Man's Orchid	Sunny site — well-drained soil	HHA	9 in.–1½ ft	July–August	6 in.–3 ft
SENECIO	Cineraria	Sun or light shade — ordinary soil	HHP	1 ft	Silvery foliage — not grown for flowers	1 ft
TAGETES	African Marigold	Sunny site — ordinary soil	HHA	1–1½ ft	June–October	1–3 ft
TAGETES	French Marigold	Sunny site — ordinary soil	HHA	6–9 in.	June–October	6 in.–1 ft
TAGETES	Tagetes	Sunny site — ordinary soil	HHA	6–9 in.	June–October	6–9 in.
VERBENA	Verbena	Sunny site — ordinary soil	HHA	1 ft ·	July–September	6 in.–1 ft
VIOLA	Pansy, Viola	Sun or light shade — ordinary soil	HA or HB	9 in.–1 ft	Varieties for all seasons	6–9 in.
ZEA	Ornamental Maize	Sunny site — moist soil	HHA	Dot plant	Coloured foliage — not grown for flowers	4–5 ft
ZINNIA	Zinnia	Sunny site — humus-rich soil	HHA	6 in.–1 ft	July–October	6 in.–2½ ft

HA = *hardy annual*   HHA = *half-hardy annual*   HB = *hardy biennial*   HHP = *half-hardy perennial*
Dot plant = *tall specimen plant with showy leaves and/or flowers*

THE BIO FRIENDLY WAY TO GROW
Bulbs

Chionodoxa luciliae

Narcissus 'La Riante'

The bulbous plants listed here include true bulbs (leaves arising from a basal plate), corms, tubers and rhizomes. The popular spring-flowering ones are known to everyone, but if you pick wisely this group can provide colour all year round.

The planting site must be well-drained and should be fairly rich in organic matter. Bone Meal is the best fertilizer but fresh manure should never be used. In damp ground Daffodils do better than Tulips. Wherever possible try to naturalise hardy bulbs by planting them in clumps around trees or on banks where they can be left to grow undisturbed. Scatter them over the ground and plant them where they fall.

The size of the bulb is all-important — buy the largest you can afford and choose ones that are plump and firm. Plant on a layer of sand — make sure that you don't leave an air pocket below the bulb. Aftercare is important. When flowering is over, the leaves must be left on the plant until they have turned yellow — don't tie Daffodil foliage into knots.

Latin name	Common name	Site & soil	Planting time	Planting depth	Spacing	Flowering period	Height
ACIDANTHERA	Acidanthera	Sunny site — well-drained soil	April	4 in.	9 in.	September	3 ft
ALLIUM	Flowering Garlic	Sunny site — well-drained soil	September –October	4–6 in.	6 in.–1 ft	June– July	9 in.–4 ft
ANEMONE BLANDA	Daisy-flowered Windflower	Sun or light shade — well-drained soil	September	2 in.	4 in.	February –April	6 in.
ANEMONE CORONARIA	Poppy-flowered Windflower	Warm and sheltered — well-drained soil	November –April	2 in.	4 in.	February –October	6–9 in.
BEGONIA	Tuberous Begonia	Light shade — moist, acid soil	June	Plant sprouted tubers	1 ft	July– September	1–1½ ft
CAMASSIA	Quamash	Sun or light shade — damp soil	September –October	4 in.	6 in.	June– July	2½–3½ ft
CANNA	Indian Shot	Sunny site — humus-rich soil	June	2 in.	1½ ft	August– October	3–4 ft
CHIONODOXA	Glory of the Snow	Sun or light shade — well-drained soil	September	3 in.	4 in.	February –March	6 in.
COLCHICUM	Autumn Crocus	Sun or light shade — well-drained soil	July– August	4 in.	9 in.	September –November	6–9 in.
CONVALLARIA	Lily of the Valley	Partial shade — damp soil	October –March	1 in.	4 in.	April –May	8 in.
CRINUM	Crinum	Sunny site — well-drained soil	April –May	10 in.	1½ ft	August– September	2–3 ft
CROCOSMIA	Montbretia	Sunny site — well-drained soil	March	3 in.	6 in.	August– September	2–3 ft
CROCUS	Crocus	Sun or light shade — well-drained soil	September –October	3 in.	4 in.	February –April	3–5 in.
CROCUS SPECIOSUS	Crocus	Sun or light shade — well-drained soil	July	3 in.	4 in.	August– October	3–5 in.
CYCLAMEN	Cyclamen	Partial shade — damp soil	July– September	2 in.	6 in.	Varieties for all seasons	3–6 in.
DAHLIA	Dahlia	Sunny site — humus-rich soil	April –May	3 in. to top of tuber	1½–3 ft	August– October	2–5 ft
ERANTHIS	Winter Aconite	Sun or light shade — well-drained soil	August– September	2 in.	3 in.	January –March	3–4 in.

Latin name	Common name	Site & soil	Planting time	Planting depth	Spacing	Flowering period	Height
ERYTHRONIUM	Dog's-tooth Violet	Partial shade — damp soil	August–October	4 in.	4 in.	March–April	6 in.
FREESIA	Outdoor Freesia	Sunny site — light soil	April	2 in.	4 in.	August–October	1 ft
FRITILLARIA IMPERIALIS	Crown Imperial	Light shade — well-drained soil	September–November	8 in.	1½ ft	April	1–3 ft
FRITILLARIA MELEAGRIS	Snake's Head Fritillary	Light shade — well-drained soil	September–November	5 in.	6 in.	April	1–3 ft
GALANTHUS	Snowdrop	Light shade — moist soil	September–October	4 in.	3 in.	January–March	5–10 in.
GALTONIA	Summer Hyacinth	Sunny site — well-drained soil	March–April	6–8 in.	1 ft	August–September	3–4 ft
GLADIOLUS	Gladiolus Hybrid	Sunny site — well-drained soil	March–May	4–5 in.	4–6 in.	July–September	1–4 ft
GLADIOLUS COLVILLII	Species Gladiolus	Sunny site — well-drained soil	October	4–5 in.	4–6 in.	April–June	2 ft
HYACINTHUS ORIENTALIS	Dutch Hyacinth	Sun or light shade — well-drained soil	September–October	6 in.	8 in.	April–May	6 in.–1 ft
HYACINTHUS O. ALBULUS	Roman Hyacinth	Sun or light shade — well-drained soil	September–October	6 in.	8 in.	March–April	6 in.–1 ft
IPHEION	Spring Starflower	Sun or light shade — well-drained soil	September–October	2 in.	4 in.	April–May	6 in.
IRIS-RETICULATA group	Dwarf Iris	Sunny site — light soil	September–October	2 in.	4 in.	January–March	4–6 in.
IRIS-XIPHIUM group	Iris	Sunny site — light soil	September–October	4–6 in.	6 in.	June–July	1–2 ft
IXIA	Corn Lily	Sunny site — light soil	March	3 in.	4 in.	June–July	1–1½ ft
LEUCOJUM AESTIVUM	Summer Snowflake	Sun or light shade — well-drained soil	August–September	4 in.	8 in.	April–May	2 ft
LEUCOJUM VERNUM	Spring Snowflake	Sun or light shade — well-drained soil	August–September	4 in.	4 in.	February–March	8 in.
LILIUM	Lily	Sun or light shade — well-drained soil	October	2–6 in. to top of bulb	6 in.–1½ ft	June–October	1–8 ft
MUSCARI	Grape Hyacinth	Sunny site — well-drained soil	September–October	3 in.	4 in.	April–May	6 in.–1 ft
NARCISSUS	Narcissus, Daffodil	Sun or light shade — well-drained soil	August–September	4–7 in.	4–8 in.	March–April	3 in.–2 ft
NERINE	Nerine	Sunny site — well-drained soil	April–May	4 in.	6 in.	September–October	2 ft
ORNITHOGALUM	Star of Bethlehem	Sun or light shade — well-drained soil	October	2 in.	4–6 in.	April–May	6 in.–1 ft
PUSCHKINIA	Striped Squill	Sun or light shade — well-drained soil	September–October	2 in.	3 in.	March–April	4 in.
RANUNCULUS	Turban Buttercup	Sunny site — well-drained soil	March–April	2 in.	6 in.	June–July	1 ft
SCILLA NONSCRIPTA	Bluebell	Sun or light shade — damp soil	August–September	4 in.	4 in.	April–June	9 in.
SCILLA SIBERICA	Siberian Squill	Sun or light shade — damp soil	August–September	4 in.	4 in.	March–April	6 in.
SPARAXIS	Harlequin Flower	Sunny site — well-drained soil	November	3 in.	4 in.	May–June	1 ft
TIGRIDIA	Tiger Flower	Sunny site — well-drained soil	April	4 in.	6 in.	July–September	1½ ft
TRITONIA	Blazing Star	Sunny site — well-drained soil	September	2 in.	6 in.	May–June	1½ ft
TULIPA	Tulip	Sunny site — well-drained soil	November–December	6 in.	5–8 in.	April–May	9 in.–2½ ft
TULIPA SPECIES	Species Tulip	Sunny site — well-drained soil	November–December	4 in.	4–6 in.	March–May	6 in.–1½ ft

THE BIO FRIENDLY WAY TO GROW
Vegetables

Crop	Sow	Plant	Harvest	Yield	Time taken (weeks)	Easy to grow	Easy to store
ASPARAGUS	Apr	Apr	May-June	25 spears/P	120 P→H	X	X
AUBERGINE	Feb ⌂	Apr ⌂	Aug-Sept	4 lb/P	20 S→H	X	X
BEAN, BROAD	Feb-Apr	—	July-Aug	10 lb/R	14 S→H	✓	X
BEAN, FRENCH	May-June	—	July-Sept	8 lb/R	10 S→H	✓	X
BEAN, RUNNER	May-June	—	Aug-Oct	30 lb/R	13 S→H	(✓)	X
	Apr ⌂	May-June	Aug-Oct	30 lb/R	14 S→H	(✓)	X
BEET, LEAF	Apr	—	Aug-Nov	7 lb/R	12 S→H	✓	X
BEETROOT	Apr-June	—	June-Oct	10 lb/R	11 S→H	✓	✓
BROCCOLI	Apr-May	June-July	Feb-May	1½ lb/P	44 S→H	(✓)	X
BRUSSELS SPROUT	Mar-Apr	May-June	Oct-Feb	2 lb/P	30 S→H	(✓)	X
CABBAGE, SPRING	July-Aug	Sept-Oct	Apr-May	¾ lb/P	35 S→H	(✓)	X
CABBAGE, SUMMER	Apr	May-June	Aug-Sept	1½ lb/P	20 S→H	(✓)	X
CABBAGE, WINTER	Apr-May	July	Nov-Feb	2½ lb/P	35 S→H	(✓)	✓
CABBAGE, CHINESE	July-Aug	—	Oct	1½ lb/P	10 S→H	✓	X
CALABRESE	Apr-May	June-July	Aug-Oct	1½ lb/P	12 S→H	(✓)	X
CAPSICUM	Feb ⌂	Apr ⌂	Aug-Sept	8 fruits/P	18 S→H	X	X
CARROT, EARLY	Mar-Apr	—	July	8 lb/R	12 S→H	(✓)	X
CARROT, MAINCROP	Apr-June	—	Sept-Oct	10 lb/R	16 S→H	(✓)	✓
CAULIFLOWER, SUMMER	Apr	June	Aug-Sept	1 lb/P	18 S→H	X	X
CAULIFLOWER, AUTUMN	Apr-May	June	Oct-Nov	2 lb/P	24 S→H	X	X
CAULIFLOWER, WINTER	May	July	Mar-May	2 lb/P	45 S→H	X	X
CELERIAC	Mar ⌂	May-June	Oct-Nov	7 lb/R	33 S→H	X	X
CELERY, TRENCH	Mar-Apr ⌂	June	Oct-Feb	12 lb/R	40 S→H	X	X
CELERY, SELF-BLANCHING	Mar-Apr ⌂	June	Aug-Oct	12 lb/R	25 S→H	X	X
CHICORY	May	—	Dec-Mar	6 lb/R	25 S→H	X	X
COURGETTE	May-June	—	July-Sept	16 fruits/P	10 S→H	(✓)	X
CUCUMBER, GREENHOUSE	Apr ⌂	May ⌂	July-Sept	25 fruits/P	12 S→H	X	X
CUCUMBER, OUTDOOR	May-June	—	Aug-Sept	10 fruits/P	12 S→H	X	X
ENDIVE	Apr-Aug	—	Sept-Feb	10 heads/R	18 S→H	X	X
KALE	May	July	Dec-Mar	2 lb/P	33 S→H	✓	X
KOHL RABI	Apr-June	—	Aug-Oct	20 globes/R	10 S→H	✓	X
LEEK	Mar-Apr	June	Nov-Mar	10 lb/R	45 S→H	(✓)	X
LETTUCE	Mar-July	—	June-Oct	15 heads/R	10 S→H	✓	X
MARROW	May-June	—	Aug-Oct	4 fruits/P	14 S→H	(✓)	✓
	Apr ⌂	June	Aug-Oct	4 fruits/P	14 S→H	X	✓
ONION, SETS	—	Mar-Apr	Aug	7 lb/R	20 P→H	✓	✓
ONION, SEED	Mar-Apr	—	Aug-Sept	8 lb/R	22 S→H	✓	✓
PARSNIP	Mar	—	Nov-Feb	8 lb/R	34 S→H	✓	✓
PEA	Mar-July	—	May-Oct	10 lb/R	12–32 S→H	X	X
POTATO, EARLY	—	Mar-Apr	June-Aug	12 lb/R	13 P→H	✓	✓
POTATO, MAINCROP	—	Apr	Sept-Oct	20 lb/R	22 P→H	✓	✓
RADISH	Mar-June	—	May-Sept	4 lb/R	6 S→H	✓	X
RHUBARB	—	Feb-Mar	Apr-July	5 lb/P	65 P→H	✓	X
SALSIFY	Apr	—	Nov-Jan	4 lb/R	25 S→H	✓	✓
SHALLOT	—	Feb-Mar	Aug	7 lb/R	20 P→H	✓	✓
SPINACH	Mar-May	—	June-Oct	6 lb/R	10 S→H	(✓)	X
SWEDE	May-June	—	Nov-Feb	30 lb/R	22 S→H	✓	✓
SWEET CORN	May	—	Aug-Sept	10 cobs/R	14 S→H	X	X
TOMATO, GREENHOUSE	Feb ⌂	Apr ⌂	July-Oct	8 lb/P	16 S→H	X	X
TOMATO, OUTDOOR	Mar-Apr ⌂	June	Aug-Sept	4 lb/P	20 S→H	X	X
TURNIP, EARLY	Mar-June	—	May-Sept	7 lb/R	8 S→H	✓	X
TURNIP, MAINCROP	July-Aug	—	Oct-Dec	12 lb/R	12 S→H	✓	✓

⌂ — under glass

P — per plant	S — sowing
R — per 10 ft row	P — planting
	H — harvesting

✓ — easy	✓ — can be stored for months
(✓) — not really easy	X — cannot be stored
X — difficult	

The months listed above are based on a location in the Midlands. Southern areas will be about 2 weeks earlier — parts of Scotland may be more than 2 weeks later.

The vegetable plot is at the centre of the organic gardening movement. For millions of people the ornamental garden is somewhere to be treated with standard fertilizers and modern sprays — lawns receive their weedkiller and Roses are protected by a systemic mildew/black spot spray which goes inside the plant. For some of these people the vegetable plot is rather different — here the plants or their produce are eaten. For this reason a natural growing system is sought. Their worries may not be based on scientific fact, but they are understandable.

What is not understandable is how so many gardeners can be so careful with what they use over and around the plants and yet be so careless with tools, glass, stakes etc. We need a Bio Friendly approach in the vegetable plot and not just organic gardening — Chapter 6 applies here as much as anywhere else in the garden.

Plan your sowings and plantings before the start of the season. You should not grow a vegetable in the same spot year after year. If you do then two basic problems are likely to occur. First, soil-living pests and diseases which thrive on the crop will rapidly increase. Secondly, the nutrient levels in the soil will become unbalanced.

The answer is to follow a crop rotation plan — a standard one is shown below. If this seems too complex do not abandon the crop rotation idea altogether. Follow a simple routine — roots this year, an above-ground crop next year and then back to a root crop.

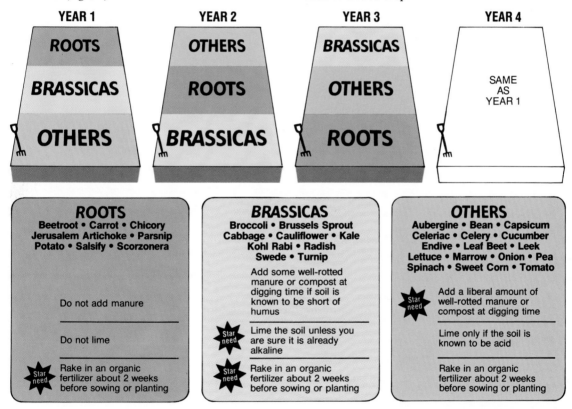

Preparing the seed bed

With some vegetables the seedlings are first raised under glass and then transplanted in the vegetable plot when conditions are suitable. This has to be done with half-hardy ones and it may be used for hardy vegetables to give them an early start.

The pattern for most vegetables, however, is to sow seeds in open ground and then leave them to grow where sown or else transplant them as seedlings to another spot where they grow to maturity. Either way, a seed bed is required.

Early spring is the usual time to start, but you must wait until the soil is workable. Use a fork or hand cultivator to break down the clods brought up by the winter digging. Do not let the prongs go deeper than 6 in. Spread an organic fertilizer (see page 37) evenly over the surface — rake into the top few inches.

Now you are ready to prepare the seed bed. Don't tramp heavily over the surface to make it smooth and level — walk over it and use a rake to break down mounds and fill in hollows.

Sowing seed

Not too early, not too deeply and not too thickly are the golden rules. Proper timing is extremely important — seeds will germinate only when the soil temperature is high enough and so there is simply no point in sowing in wet and near-freezing soil.

Draw out the drill with a stick, trowel or edge of a hoe. Water *gently* if the bottom of the drill is dry. Sprinkle seed along the drill — use thumb and forefinger to apply the seed.

Cover the seed by gently replacing the soil with the back of a rake. If you are not skilled at this operation push the soil back with your fingers. Firm gently but do not water. Cover the surface with newspaper if the weather is dry.

Thinning

Despite the often-repeated recommendation to sow thinly you will usually find that the emerged seedlings are too close together. Thinning is necessary, and this is a job to be tackled as soon as the plants are large enough to handle. Hold down the soil around the unwanted seedling with one hand and pull it up with the other. If the seedlings are too close together to allow this technique, merely nip off the top growth. Firm the soil around the remaining seedlings after thinning and water gently. Thinning is usually carried out in stages.

Feeding

A base dressing will have been applied during the spring preparation of the plot. Crops which take some time to mature will need one or more top dressings during the growing season. Use a well-balanced natural fertilizer such as Bio Friendly Plant Food — make sure the soil is moist before applying the fertilizer and hoe or lightly rake in afterwards.

Weeding

The basic techniques for keeping weeds in check are hoeing, mulching and hand pulling — read the section on page 49. Never let weeds get out of hand — apart from making the plot look untidy and competing with the crops weeds can harbour pests and diseases. Remove the roots of perennial weeds at digging and seed bed preparation time, but no matter how thoroughly you do this you will find that additional weeds will appear among the growing crops.

Hoe regularly and in the proper way if a mulch has not been used. Make sure you keep away from stems and do not go deeper than an inch below the surface. Of course a hoe is of little use if you have taken over a neglected allotment or vegetable plot which is a sea of weeds. For the chemical gardener a non-selective weedkiller over the whole area is the answer — for the Bio Friendly gardener the best way to tackle the problem is to use a weed control mulch (see page 9).

Growing vegetables in beds rather than rows reduces the weed problem quite significantly — see page 29.

Mulching

Mulching is an in-season method of manuring —see page 9 for full details. Although primarily used in the herbaceous border, fruit garden and shrub border, this technique has a part to play in the vegetable plot. The soil is enriched with humus-making material — a vital step if you have a no-digging garden.

Spraying

People who claim that they *never* need to spray are lying, lucky or living on poor vegetables. Both pests and diseases attack well-grown as well as sickly plants. Strength and vigour help but do not produce immunity in plants any more than in humans. Most of these problems can be ignored — they may be unsightly but do an amount of harm which is acceptable. There are a few pests, however, where something must be done or the crop will be ruined. The answer depends on the area involved. For a small plot a ready-to-use horticultural soap (Bio Friendly Pest Pistol) is the most convenient way to kill pests without harming beneficial insects — for a larger area you will need a sprayer containing a derris + quassia formulation such as Bio Friendly Pest Spray.

Protecting crops

Glass cloche   Plastic cloche

Glass cloches will warm up the soil before planting or sowing in the spring, and then protect the young plants from wind and rain. Glass is effective in trapping the sun's rays and so raising the temperature of the soil and plants, but it is also dangerous. Do take care when storing and handling. If children play regularly in the area you should seriously consider using plastic instead of glass. Polythene and PVC are less effective in creating a greenhouse effect but are much safer. With all cloches some ventilation must be provided — increase the amount as temperatures rise. Provide ventilation by leaving gaps between cloches, not by leaving the ends open. There is no need to remove the cloches before watering.

Crop	Row System		Bed System	
	Distance between rows (in.)	Distance between plants (in.)	Distance between rows (in.)	Distance between plants (in.)
BEAN, BROAD	8–24	8	6	6
BEAN, FRENCH	18	4	6	6
BEAN, RUNNER	18–24	9	Not recommended	
BEETROOT	12	4	3	3
BROCCOLI	18	18	15	15
BRUSSELS SPROUT	30	30	18	18
CABBAGE	18	18	15	15
CARROT	6	3	6	3
CAULIFLOWER	18	24	18	18
CUCUMBER	24	24	24	24
KALE	18	18	15	15
LEEK	12	6	6	6
LETTUCE	12	12	9	9
ONION	9	4	2	2
PEA	24	2	Not recommended	
RADISH	6	2	2	2
SPINACH	12	6	6	6
SWEDE	15	9	9	9
TOMATO	30	18	18	18
TURNIP	12	9	9	9

THE BED SYSTEM

The instructions in most books and on seed packets are for the traditional row method of growing vegetables. The relatively wide spaces between the rows allow passage so that weeding, watering, spraying etc can be carried out.

A new alternative for many types is the bed system, and its popularity continues to grow. Each vegetable is sown in a block so that all the plants are the same distance from each other — the spacings are quite close so that the leaves of adjacent plants touch when the plants are mature. See page 29 for full details.

THE BIO FRIENDLY WAY TO GROW
Herbaceous Perennials

Echinacea purpurea
'Bressingham Hybrid'

The herbaceous border is in some ways the star of the Bio Friendly movement. It is certainly friendly to human beings as it is not one of the danger areas, and it is friendly to wildlife — the wide range of flowers and the presence of seedheads make it attractive to birds, butterflies etc.

The problem is that this kind of border requires a great deal of space and attention, and it also looks dull for much of the year. For the average-sized garden the mixed border is a better idea. Roses, conifers, evergreens and flowering shrubs form the permanent skeleton — herbaceous perennials are planted in groups of three or five between them. Annuals and bulbs fill in the bare spots.

Plant perennials in early spring. Apply a dressing of an organic fertilizer every year before putting down a humus mulch (see page 9) in early May. Water if the weather is dry — lack of moisture encourages mildew. Support is often needed — in most cases tying to a single stake should be avoided. For bushy plants use instead three or four twiggy sticks and twine.

Hemerocallis
'Golden Chimes'

Latin name	Common name	Site & soil	Propagation	Notes
ACANTHUS	Bear's Breeches	Sun or light shade — well-drained soil	Divide clumps — autumn	A. spinosus is the usual one — height 4 ft, spacing 2½ ft, flowers July–September. Blooms are white lipped and purple hooded
ACHILLEA	Yarrow	Sunny site — well-drained soil	Divide clumps — autumn	A. filipendulina Gold Plate bears flat-topped yellow flower-heads — height 4½ ft, spacing 2 ft, flowers June–September
AGAPANTHUS	African Lily	Sunny site — humus-rich soil	Divide clumps — spring	Large head of blue flowers above strap-like leaves. Height 2½ ft, spacing 2 ft, flowers July–September. Not fully hardy
AJUGA	Bugle	Sun or light shade — ordinary soil	Divide clumps — autumn	A creeping plant — grow a variety with coloured leaves — bronze, purple, cream etc. Height 4 in., spacing 15 in., flowers May–August
ALCHEMILLA	Lady's Mantle	Sun or light shade — well-drained soil	Divide clumps — spring	A. mollis is an old favourite — height 1½ ft, spacing 1½ ft, flowers June–August. Blooms small, greenish-yellow
ALSTROEMERIA	Peruvian Lily	Sunny site — fertile soil	Sow seeds — spring	Large trumpets (2 in. across) in loose clusters. Many hybrids available — height 2 ft, spacing 1½ ft, flowers June–August
ANCHUSA	Alkanet	Sunny site — well-drained soil	Divide clumps — spring	Grown for its vivid blue flowers — a straggly short-lived plant. Choose an A. azurea variety — height 1½–5 ft, flowers June–August
ANEMONE	Japanese Anemone	Sun or light shade — well-drained soil	Divide clumps — spring	Saucer-shaped blooms (2 in. across) and deeply-lobed leaves. Height 2–4 ft, spacing 1–1½ ft, flowers August–October
AQUILEGIA	Columbine	Partial shade — well-drained soil	Divide clumps — autumn	Old cottage-garden favourite. Choose a modern hybrid — height 1½–3 ft, spacing 1 ft, flowers May–June
ASTER	Michaelmas Daisy	Sunny site — well-drained soil	Divide clumps — spring	Scores of varieties available — white, red, blue, pink and mauve. Height 2–5 ft, spacing 1½ ft, flowers August–October
ASTILBE	Astilbe	Light shade — moist soil	Divide clumps — spring	Feathery plumes of tiny flowers. Many varieties of A. arendsii can be bought — height 2–3 ft, spacing 1½ ft, flowers June–August
BERGENIA	Large-leaved Saxifrage	Sun or light shade — well-drained soil	Divide clumps — autumn	Easy-to-grow ground cover. Fleshy leaves, hyacinth-like flower-spikes. Height 1½ ft, spacing 1½ ft, flowers March–April
BRUNNERA	Perennial Forget-me-not	Partial shade — well-drained soil	Divide clumps — autumn	Easy-to-grow ground cover. Heart-shaped leaves, myosotis-like blooms. Height 1½ ft, spacing 1½ ft, flowers April–June
CALTHA	Marsh Marigold	Sun or light shade — moist soil	Divide clumps — after flowering	Golden flowers (1–2 in. across) above dark green leaves. Height 1 ft, spacing 1 ft, flowers April–June
CAMPANULA	Bellflower	Sun or light shade — well-drained soil	Cuttings — spring	Blooms bell-like or star-shaped — white or blue. Several species available — height 2–5 ft, spacing 1–1½ ft, flowers June–August
CHRYSANTHEMUM	Chrysanthemum	Sunny site — well-drained soil	Cuttings — spring	Raised afresh each year from cuttings. Hundreds of varieties available — all colours except blue. See The Flower Expert for details

Latin name	Common name	Site & soil	Propagation	Notes
CHRYSANTHEMUM	Shasta Daisy	Sunny site — non-acid soil	Divide clumps — spring	C. maximum is the hardy Chrysanthemum. Many named varieties available — height 2½–3 ft, spacing 1½ ft, flowers June–August
COREOPSIS	Tickseed	Sun or light shade — well-drained soil	Sow seeds — spring	Yellow daisy-like flowers on slender stalks. C. grandiflora is the usual species — height 1½ ft, spacing 1½ ft, flowers June–September
CORTADERIA	Pampas Grass	Sun or light shade — well-drained soil	Buy	Silvery plumes about 1½ ft long on tall stalks. Grow a variety of C. selloana — height 4–10 ft, flowers October
DELPHINIUM	Delphinium	Sunny site — well-drained soil	Divide clumps — spring	Dwarfs and giants available in white, blue, pink, mauve and purple. Height 3–8 ft, spacing 1½–2½ ft, flowers June–July
DIANTHUS	Border Carnation	Sunny site — non-acid soil	Cuttings — summer	Enormous list of varieties — all sorts of colours. Height 2–3 ft, spacing 1½ ft, flowers July–August. Petals smooth-edged
DIANTHUS	Pinks	Sunny site — non-acid soil	Cuttings — summer	Old-fashioned and modern varieties available — smaller and daintier than Carnations. Height 1–1½ ft, spacing 1 ft, flowers June–July
DICENTRA	Bleeding Heart	Light shade — well-drained soil	Divide clumps — autumn	Most popular Dicentra is also the largest — D. spectabilis. Height 2–3 ft, spacing 1½ ft, flowers May–June
DORONICUM	Leopard's Bane	Sun or light shade — well-drained soil	Divide clumps — autumn	Varieties of D. plantagineum are usually chosen — height 2–3 ft, spacing 1½ ft, flowers April–June. Large daisy-like blooms
ECHINACEA	Purple Coneflower	Sunny site — well-drained soil	Divide clumps — spring	E. purpurea is the species to grow — height 3–4 ft, spacing 2 ft, flowers July–October. Pink or purple petals
ECHINOPS	Globe Thistle	Sunny site — well-drained soil	Divide clumps — spring	Globular flower-heads above thistle-like leaves. For the back of the border — height 3–5 ft, spacing 2 ft, flowers July–September
ERIGERON	Fleabane	Sun or light shade — well-drained soil	Divide clumps — spring	Looks like a small Michaelmas Daisy — height 1–2 ft, spacing 1 ft, flowers June–August. Pink, blue and lilac available
ERYNGIUM	Sea Holly	Sunny site — well-drained soil	Divide clumps — spring	Thimble-shaped blue flowers above thistle-like leaves. Several species available — height 1½–3 ft, spacing 1–1½ ft, flowers July–September
EUPHORBIA	Spurge	Sun or light shade — well-drained soil	Cuttings — spring	Flower colour is nearly always yellow or green, but there is a bright orange one. Height 2½ ft, spacing 1½ ft, flowers May
FUCHSIA	Fuchsia	Sun or light shade — well-drained soil	Cuttings — summer	Hundreds of named hybrids are available — a few are hardy but most are treated as summer bedding plants. Flowers 2–4 in. long
GAILLARDIA	Blanket Flower	Sunny site — avoid heavy soil	Divide clumps — spring	Popular — large daisy-like blooms (2–4 in. across) in yellow and red. Height 1½–2½ ft, spacing 1½ ft, flowers June–September
GERANIUM	Crane's-bill	Sun or light shade — well-drained soil	Divide clumps — spring	Useful ground cover — saucer-shaped flowers in white, pink, blue or red. Height 1–2 ft, spacing 1½ ft, flowers May–August
GEUM	Avens	Sun or light shade — well-drained soil	Divide clumps — spring	An old favourite — bright, bowl-shaped blooms on top of wiry stems. Height 1–2 ft, spacing 1½ ft, flowers May–September
GYPSOPHILA	Baby's Breath	Sun or light shade — non-acid soil	Cuttings — summer	Tiny white or pale pink flowers form a billowy cloud above thin stems. Height 3 ft, spacing 3 ft, flowers June–August
HELENIUM	Sneezewort	Sun or light shade — well-drained soil	Divide clumps — autumn	Bronze-red H. autumnale Moerheim Beauty is the popular one — height 3 ft, spacing 2 ft, flowers July–September. Yellow varieties available
HELLEBORUS	Christmas Rose	Partial shade — moist soil	Buy	H. niger bears large, saucer-shaped blooms — white with golden stamens. Height 1–1½ ft, spacing 1½ ft, flowers January–March
HELLEBORUS	Lenten Rose	Partial shade — moist soil	Buy	H. orientalis bears large, saucer-shaped blooms — white, pink or purple. Height 1–1½ ft, spacing 1½ ft, flowers February–April
HEMEROCALLIS	Day Lily	Sun or light shade — ordinary soil	Divide clumps — autumn	Large lily-like trumpets in shades from pale yellow to rich red. Many varieties — height 3 ft, spacing 2 ft, flowers June–August
HEUCHERA	Coral Flower	Sun or light shade — well-drained soil	Divide clumps — autumn	Tiny bell-shaped blooms on top of slender stems. Height 1½–2½ ft, spacing 1½ ft, flowers June–August. White, pink or red
HOSTA	Plantain Lily	Partial shade — ordinary soil	Divide clumps — spring	Useful ground cover grown for its spikes of flowers and its attractive foliage. Height 1½–3 ft, spacing 2 ft, flowers July–August
INCARVILLEA	Chinese Trumpet Flower	Sunny site — well-drained soil	Sow seeds — spring	Large trumpets in clusters appear before the leaves. Height 1–2 ft, spacing 1 ft, flowers May–June. Pale or deep pink
IRIS	Iris	Sunny site — well-drained soil	Divide rhizomes — late summer	Bearded types (fleshy hairs on petals) dominate the catalogue lists. Height 9 in.–3 ft, spacing 1 ft, flowers April–June, depending on variety
KNIPHOFIA	Red Hot Poker	Sunny site — well-drained soil	Divide clumps — spring	Usual choice is a variety or hybrid of K. uvaria — height 2½–5 ft, spacing 3 ft, flowers July–September. Various colour combinations
LIATRIS	Gayfeather	Sun or light shade — moist soil	Divide clumps — spring	Unusual flower-spike feature — blooms open from top downwards. Height 1½ ft, spacing 1½ ft, flowers August–September
LIGULARIA	Ligularia	Partial shade — moist soil	Divide clumps — autumn	Useful ground cover with large leaves and yellow or orange daisy-like blooms. Height 3–4 ft, spacing 2½ ft, flowers July–September
LINUM	Perennial Flax	Sunny site — well-drained soil	Sow seeds — spring	Short-lived blooms on wiry stems — blue is the most popular colour. Height 1–2 ft, spacing 1 ft, flowers June–August
LUPINUS	Lupin	Sun or light shade — well-drained soil	Sow seeds — spring	Russell hybrids provide stately spires of blooms in a vast range of colours — height 3–4 ft, spacing 2 ft, flowers June–July

Latin name	Common name	Site & soil	Propagation	Notes
LYCHNIS	Campion	Sunny site — well-drained soil	Divide clumps — autumn	L. chalcedonica (Jerusalem Cross) is the one to grow — large heads of red blooms. Height 3 ft, spacing 1½ ft, flowers June–August
LYTHRUM	Purple Loosestrife	Sun or light shade — moist soil	Divide clumps — autumn	Long and narrow flower-spikes, pink or red. Basic species is L. salicaria — height 2½–5 ft, spacing 1½ ft, flowers June–September
MACLEAYA	Plume Poppy	Sun or light shade — ordinary soil	Divide clumps — autumn	Space is needed for the bronzy leaves and tall plumes of pinkish flowers. Height 6–8 ft, spacing 3 ft, flowers July–August
MECONOPSIS	Meconopsis	Light shade — humus-rich soil	Sow seeds — spring	Both the blue Himalayan Poppy (3 ft) and yellow Welsh Poppy (1 ft) belong here. Flowering period June–August
MONARDA	Bergamot	Sun or light shade — moist soil	Divide clumps — spring	Grow one of the named hybrids of M. didyma — height 2–3 ft, spacing 2 ft, flowers June–September
NEPETA	Catmint	Sunny site — ordinary soil	Divide clumps — spring	Popular edging plant — small lavender flowers and aromatic greyish leaves. Height 1–3 ft, spacing 1½ ft, flowers May–September
OENOTHERA	Evening Primrose	Sunny site — well-drained soil	Divide clumps — spring	Yellow poppy-like blooms — O. missouriensis bears the largest. Height 6 in.–1½ ft, spacing 1–1½ ft, flowers July–September
PAEONIA	Paeony	Sunny site — well-drained soil	Buy	Vast bowls of petals up to 7 in. across — single, double or anemone-flowered. Height 1½–3 ft, spacing 1½–2 ft, flowers April–July
PAPAVER	Oriental Poppy	Sunny site — well-drained soil	Divide clumps — spring	Bowl-shaped flowers up to 6 in. across. Many named varieties available — height 3 ft, spacing 1½ ft, flowers May–June
PELARGONIUM	Geranium	Sunny site — well-drained soil	Cuttings — summer	Height 1–2 ft, spacing 1 ft. Two basic types — Bedding Geraniums (flowers ½–1 in. across) and Regal Geraniums (frilled flowers 1½–2 in. across)
PENSTEMON	Beard Tongue	Sunny site — well-drained soil	Cuttings — summer	Grow a named hybrid — height 1½–2 ft, spacing 1 ft, flowers June–September. Red is the usual colour. Not fully hardy
PHLOX	Phlox	Sun or light shade — moist soil	Divide clumps — spring	Large trusses of flat-faced flowers. The most popular Phlox is P. paniculata — height 2–4 ft, spacing 1½ ft, flowers July–October
PHYSALIS	Chinese Lantern	Sun or light shade — ordinary soil	Divide clumps — spring	Grown for 2 in. long 'lanterns' — useful for drying. Height 2 ft, spacing 3 ft, fruits September–October. Gold- or flame-coloured
PLATYCODON	Balloon Flower	Sun or light shade — well-drained soil	Buy	Unusual flower feature — buds swell into large, angular balloons before opening. Height 1–2 ft, spacing 1 ft, flowers June–September
POLEMONIUM	Jacob's Ladder	Sun or light shade — well-drained soil	Divide clumps — autumn	An old cottage-garden plant — choose a modern variety if space is limited. Height 1–3 ft, spacing 1 ft, flowers June–August
POLYGONATUM	Solomon's Seal	Shade — ordinary soil	Divide clumps — autumn	Thrives under trees and shrubs — green-tipped white blooms in pendent clusters. Height 2–3 ft, spacing 2 ft, flowers May–June
POLYGONUM	Knotweed	Sun or light shade — ordinary soil	Divide clumps — autumn	Evergreen ground cover — pokers of pink flowers. Choose a P. affine variety — height 1 ft, spacing 2 ft, flowers June–October
POTENTILLA	Cinquefoil	Sunny site — well-drained soil	Divide clumps — spring	Bright saucer-shaped flowers in reds and yellows. Several named hybrids — height 1–2 ft, spacing 1½ ft, flowers June–September
PRIMULA	Primrose	Partial shade — humus-rich soil	Divide clumps — spring	Many species and hybrids are available — Pacific Strain of Polyanthus most popular. Height 1 ft, spacing 1 ft, flowers March–May
PYRETHRUM	Feverfew	Sunny site — well-drained soil	Divide clumps — spring	Single or double daisy-like blooms 2 in. across — usual colours pink and red. Height 2–3 ft, spacing 1½ ft, flowers May–June
RUDBECKIA	Coneflower	Sun or light shade — ordinary soil	Divide clumps — spring	Dark-centred, star-shaped blooms. Popular variety is R. fulgida Goldsturm — height 2 ft, spacing 2 ft, flowers July–September
SALVIA	Perennial Sage	Sun or light shade — well-drained soil	Divide clumps — autumn	Blue — not red like the Annual Salvia. Usual species is S. superba — height 3 ft, spacing 1½ ft, flowers July–September
SAXIFRAGA	Saxifrage	Partial shade — humus-rich soil	Divide clumps — spring	Starry flowers above rosettes or clumps of leaves. Popular one is London Pride — height 1 ft, spacing 1½ ft, flowers May–July
SCABIOSA	Scabious	Sunny site — non-acid soil	Divide clumps — spring	Flowers are frilly-edged pincushions up to 4 in. across. Basic species is S. caucasica — height 2–3 ft, spacing 1½ ft, flowers June–October
SEDUM	Stonecrop	Sunny site — well-drained soil	Divide clumps — spring	The popular Ice Plant is S. spectabile — height 1–2 ft, spacing 1 ft, flowers August–October. Flower-heads 4–6 in. across
SOLIDAGO	Golden Rod	Sun or light shade — well-drained soil	Divide clumps — spring	Feathery flower-heads above narrow leaves. Choose a named hybrid — height 1–7 ft, spacing 1–2 ft, flowers July–September
STACHYS	Lamb's Ears	Sun or light shade — well-drained soil	Divide clumps — autumn	The popular Stachys is Lamb's Ears (S. lanata) — height 1½ ft, spacing 1 ft, flowers July–August. Woolly foliage, pale purple blooms
TRADESCANTIA	Spiderwort	Sun or light shade — ordinary soil	Divide clumps — spring	Silky three-petalled blooms above sword-like leaves. The species is T. virginiana — height 1½–2 ft, spacing 1½ ft, flowers June–September
TROLLIUS	Globe Flower	Sun or light shade — moist soil	Divide clumps — autumn	Buttercup-like blooms 2 in. across. Hybrids range from pale cream to dark orange — height 1½–2½ ft, spacing 1½ ft, flowers May–June
VERBASCUM	Mullein	Sunny site — well-drained soil	Root cuttings — winter	Branched flower-spikes above woolly leaves. Choose a named variety — many colours available. Height 3–6 ft, spacing 2 ft, flowers June–August
VERONICA	Speedwell	Sun or light shade — well-drained soil	Divide clumps — autumn	Narrow spikes of blue or white blooms. Size of varieties covers a wide range — height 1–5 ft, spacing 1–2 ft, flowers May–June

THE BIO FRIENDLY WAY TO GROW

Trees, Shrubs & Climbers

Rhododendron 'Mrs G.W. Leak'

Woody plants have a special place in the Bio Friendly garden. The plot is given an air of permanence and maturity — many forms of wildlife are provided with a home. Most trees, however, are too large for the average garden, the range and use of climbers are limited and none of the conifers produce a floral display. The shrubs have none of these drawbacks — there is an abundance of varieties for gardens of every size.

Growing shrubs is one of the most interesting and rewarding aspects of gardening. There are three basic rules to remember — choose sensibly, plant properly and then prune correctly. Choose a selection of unusual types and common-or-garden varieties, including both early- and late-flowering sorts. Plant with a mixture of soil, peat and Bone Meal — don't put the shrubs too closely together. Finally, look up the correct time to prune each plant — cutting too early or too little can result in a poor display of flowers.

Santolina chamaecyparissus

Latin name	Common name	Site & soil	Type	Pruning	Propagation	Notes
ACER	Japanese Maple	Partial shade — acid soil	S:D	Not necessary	Buy	Varieties of A. palmatum grown for leaf shape and colour
ARUNDINARIA	Bamboo	Partial shade — ordinary soil	S:E	Not necessary	Divide clumps — autumn	Varieties range from 3–20 ft tall
AUCUBA	Aucuba	Sun or shade — ordinary soil	S:E	Not necessary	Cuttings — summer	Popular — planted where little else will grow
BERBERIS	Barberry	Sun or light shade — ordinary soil	S: D or E	Not necessary	Cuttings — summer	Popular and easy — range from 2–9 ft tall
BETULA	Birch	Sun or light shade — ordinary soil	T:D	Remove dead wood — spring	Buy	B. pendula (Silver Birch) is the popular one
BUDDLEIA	Butterfly Bush	Sunny site — well-drained soil	S: D or semi E	Popular varieties — cut back in March	Cuttings — autumn	Types bearing floral cones need annual pruning
BUXUS	Box	Sun or light shade — ordinary soil	S:E	Not necessary	Cuttings — summer	An excellent hedging or tub plant. Small glossy leaves
CALLUNA	Heather	Sunny site — acid soil	S:E	Lightly trim — March	Cuttings — summer	Hundreds of named varieties — 9–24 in. high
CAMELLIA	Camellia	Sun or light shade — acid soil	S:E	Not necessary	Cuttings — summer	Should be more popular — large blooms in March–May
CEANOTHUS	Californian Lilac	Sunny site — well-drained soil	S: D or E	D types — cut back in March	Cuttings — summer	Evergreen varieties are not fully hardy. Plant in spring
CHAENOMELES	Japonica	Sun or light shade — ordinary soil	S:D	Not necessary	Plant rooted suckers	Old favourite, grown for spring flowers and autumn fruits
CHOISYA	Mexican Orange	Sunny site — ordinary soil	S:E	Not necessary	Cuttings — summer	Fragrant plant — white, starry flowers in May
CISTUS	Rock Rose	Sunny site — well-drained soil	S:E	Not necessary	Cuttings — summer	Succession of papery flowers throughout June and July
CLEMATIS	Virgin's Bower	Sun on stems — fertile soil	C: D or E	Complicated. Depends on variety	Cuttings — summer	The large-flowered hybrids are the ones usually grown
CORNUS	Dogwood	Sun or light shade — ordinary soil	S:D	Bark types — cut back in March	Cuttings — autumn	Varieties chosen for coloured bark or floral display
CORYLUS	Hazel	Sunny site — ordinary soil	T:D	Remove some old wood — spring	Plant rooted suckers	Choose a variety with colourful foliage (yellow or purple)
COTINUS	Smoke Bush	Sunny site — ordinary soil	S:D	Remove unwanted growth — spring	Plant rooted suckers	Feathery flower-heads — sold under old name Rhus cotinus
COTONEASTER	Cotoneaster	Sun or light shade — ordinary soil	S: D or E	Not necessary	Cuttings — summer	All shapes and sizes from ground covers to 20 ft bushes

S: = shrub   T: = tree   C: = climber   D = deciduous   E = evergreen

Latin name	Common name	Site & soil	Type	Pruning	Propagation	Notes
CRATAEGUS	Hawthorn	Sun or light shade — ordinary soil	T:D	Not necessary	Buy	White, red or pink flowers in May — berries in autumn
CYTISUS	Broom	Sunny site — sandy soil	S: D or E	Trim back — after flowering	Cuttings — summer	Flowers clothe long whippy branches in May or June
DAPHNE	Daphne	Sunny site — humus-rich soil	S: D or E	Not necessary	Cuttings — summer	Popular species is D. mezereum — purplish flowers in February
DEUTZIA	Deutzia	Sun or light shade — ordinary soil	S:D	Cut back — after flowering	Cuttings — autumn	White or pink flowers borne freely in June
ELAEAGNUS	Oleaster	Sun or light shade — ordinary soil	S: D or E	Not necessary	Plant rooted suckers	Popular variety is yellow-splashed E. pungens Maculata
ERICA	Heather	Sun or light shade — well-drained soil	S:E	Lightly trim — after flowering	Cuttings — summer	Varieties available for flowering at any season and for chalky soil
ESCALLONIA	Escallonia	Sun or light shade — ordinary soil	S:E	Cut back — autumn	Cuttings — summer	Useful as a hedge, especially in coastal areas
EUCALYPTUS	Gum Tree	Sunny site — avoid sandy soil	T:E	Cut back — spring	Buy	Regular pruning maintains round and waxy blue foliage
EUONYMUS	Euonymus	Sun or light shade — ordinary soil	S: D or E	Not necessary	Cuttings — summer	The popular ones are the evergreens — excellent ground cover
FAGUS	Beech	Sun or light shade — avoid heavy soil	T:D	Trim back — summer	Buy	Choose a variety of F. sylvatica — purple, copper and yellow available
FORSYTHIA	Forsythia	Sun or light shade — ordinary soil	S:D	Cut back shoots with faded blooms	Cuttings — autumn	Very popular — yellow flowers in March and April
FUCHSIA	Fuchsia	Sun or light shade — fertile soil	S:D	Cut back — March	Cuttings — summer	Choose a hardy variety. Pendent bells July-October
GARRYA	Silk Tassel Bush	Sun or light shade — ordinary soil	S:E	Not necessary	Cuttings — summer	Long and slender catkins drape bushes January-February
GENISTA	Broom	Sunny site — avoid heavy soil	S:D	Cut back shoots with faded blooms	Seed	Pea-like yellow flowers in June. Avoid feeding
HAMAMELIS	Witch Hazel	Sun or light shade — well-drained soil	S:D	Not necessary	Buy	Fragrant flowers appear before leaves in winter
HEBE	Veronica	Sun or light shade — ordinary soil	S:E	Not necessary	Cuttings — summer	Small varieties, such as Autumn Glory, are completely hardy
HEDERA	Ivy	Shady site — ordinary soil	C:E	Not necessary	Plant rooted runners	Many colourful varieties are available — yellow, golden etc
HELIANTHEMUM	Rock Rose	Sunny site — well-drained soil	S:E	Cut back — after flowering	Cuttings — summer	Succession of flowers May-July. Avoid feeding
HYDRANGEA	Hydrangea	Partial shade — well-drained soil	S:D	Remove flower-heads — March	Cuttings — summer	Many Lacecap and Mophead varieties are available
HYPERICUM	St. John's Wort	Sun or shade — ordinary soil	S: E or semi E	Cut back — March	Cuttings — summer	Excellent yellow-flowered shrubs — usually grown as ground cover
ILEX	Holly	Sun or shade — ordinary soil	S:E	Trim back — spring or summer	Cuttings — autumn	Wide range of leaf and berry colours. Always buy small plants
JASMINUM	Winter Jasmine	Sun or light shade — ordinary soil	S:D	Cut back shoots with faded blooms	Cuttings — summer	J. nudiflorum is an old favourite — yellow flowers November-February
KALMIA	Calico Bush	Partial shade — acid soil	S:E	Not necessary	Cuttings — summer	Rhododendron-like bush — pink flowers in June
KERRIA	Jew's Mallow	Sun or light shade — ordinary soil	S:D	Cut back shoots with faded blooms	Plant rooted suckers	Popular and easy — yellow flowers in April and May
LABURNUM	Golden Rain	Sun or light shade — ordinary soil	T:D	Remove dead wood — summer	Buy	Long sprays of flowers in May or June
LAURUS	Bay Laurel	Sun or light shade — ordinary soil	S:E	Trim back — spring	Cuttings — summer	L. nobilis grows up to 20 ft — leaves scorched by frost
LAVANDULA	Lavender	Sun or light shade — well-drained soil	S:E	Trim back — spring	Cuttings — autumn	Flowers appear in July-September — white, pink, blue or lavender
LIGUSTRUM	Privet	Sun or shade — ordinary soil	S: E or semi E	Trim back — May and August	Cuttings — autumn	Often regarded with contempt, but there are colourful varieties
LONICERA	Honeysuckle	Sun or light shade — fertile soil	C: D or semi E	Cut back some stems — after flowering	Cuttings — summer	Most varieties have fragrant blooms — June-August
MAGNOLIA	Magnolia	Sun or light shade — humus-rich soil	S: D or E	Not necessary	Layer stems — summer	Beautiful flowers (white, pink or red) on 4-20 ft plants
MAHONIA	Mahonia	Partial shade — ordinary soil	S:E	Not necessary	Plant rooted suckers	Useful yellow-flowered shrubs — popular under trees as ground cover

S: = *shrub*   T: = *tree*   C: = *climber*   D = *deciduous*   E = *evergreen*

Latin name	Common name	Site & soil	Type	Pruning	Propagation	Notes
MALUS	Flowering Crab	Sunny site — well-drained soil	T:D	Remove dead wood — winter	Buy	Flowers in April or May — colourful fruits in autumn
PARTHENOCISSUS	Virginia Creeper	Sun or light shade — fertile soil	C:D	Remove unwanted growth — spring	Layer stems — autumn	Leaves turn red in autumn. Popular one is P. tricuspidata
PERNETTYA	Prickly Heath	Sun or light shade — acid soil	S:E	Trim back — summer	Plant rooted suckers	Large, porcelain-like berries throughout the winter
PHILADELPHUS	Mock Orange	Sun or light shade — ordinary soil	S:D	Cut back some shoots	Cuttings — autumn	White fragrant flowers in June and July. Wrongly called Syringa
PIERIS	Andromeda	Partial shade — acid soil	S:E	Not necessary	Layer stems — summer	Bright red new growth in spring. White floral sprays
POLYGONUM	Russian Vine	Sun or light shade — ordinary soil	C:D	Remove unwanted growth — spring	Cuttings — summer	Fast-growing, twining climber. Popular one is P. baldschuanicum
POPULUS	Poplar	Sun or light shade — ordinary soil	T:D	Remove dead wood — summer	Buy	Very quick growing — not for small gardens
POTENTILLA	Shrubby Cinquefoil	Sun or light shade — well-drained soil	S:D	Cut back old stems — March	Cuttings — summer	Noted for length of flowering season — May-September
PRUNUS	Prunus	Sun or light shade — ordinary soil	S: D or E	Trim — late spring (E), late summer (D)	Cuttings (E) — summer	Evergreens include Cherry Laurel and Portugal Laurel. Useful hedging plants
PRUNUS	Ornamental Cherry/Peach	Sunny site — ordinary soil	T:D	Remove dead wood — summer	Buy	Very popular — usual choice is a Japanese Cherry
PYRACANTHA	Firethorn	Sun or light shade — ordinary soil	S:E	Cut back — after flowering	Cuttings — summer	Grown for massed display of red or yellow berries in autumn
RHODODENDRON	Azalea	Partial shade — acid soil	S: D or E	Remove dead flowers	Layer stems — summer	Daintier than garden 'Rhododendron'. Deciduous types taller than evergreens
RHODODENDRON	Rhododendron	Partial shade — acid soil	S:E	Remove dead flowers	Buy	Very popular — usual height 4–6 ft, usual flowering month May
RHUS	Sumach	Sunny site — ordinary soil	S:D	Cut stems to 1 ft — February	Plant rooted suckers	Grown for their brilliant foliage colours in autumn. Large flower-spikes
RIBES	Flowering Currant	Sun or light shade — ordinary soil	S: D or semi E	Cut back shoots with faded blooms	Cuttings — autumn	R. sanguineum is seen everywhere. Pink or red flowers in pendent heads
ROBINIA	False Acacia	Sun or light shade — ordinary soil	T:D	Remove dead wood — summer	Buy	R. pseudoacacia Frisia is outstanding — layers of golden foliage
SALIX	Willow	Sun or light shade — deep soil	T:D	Not necessary	Buy	Ordinary Weeping Willow too large for average gardens
SANTOLINA	Lavender Cotton	Sunny site — well-drained soil	S:D	Trim back — after flowering	Cuttings — summer	Yellow, button-like flowers (June–August) and silvery foliage
SENECIO	Senecio	Sunny site — well-drained soil	S:E	Not necessary	Cuttings — summer	Yellow, daisy-like flowers (June) and leathery foliage
SKIMMIA	Skimmia	Partial shade — acid soil	S:E	Not necessary	Cuttings — summer	You will need male and female plants of S. japonica for red berries
SORBUS	Mountain Ash	Sun or light shade — ordinary soil	T:D	Not necessary	Buy	White flowers in May and red or yellow berries in autumn
SPARTIUM	Spanish Broom	Sunny site — well-drained soil	S:D	Trim back last year's growth — March	Cuttings — summer	Yellow flowers, rush-like stems. Keep in check by regular pruning
SPIRAEA	Spiraea	Sun or light shade — fertile soil	S:D	Cut back summer types — March	Cuttings — autumn	Spring-flowering varieties white — summer-flowering ones pink or red
SYMPHORICARPOS	Snowberry	Sun or shade — ordinary soil	S:D	Trim back — summer	Plant rooted suckers	Rampant grower — marble-like berries in October
SYRINGA	Lilac	Sunny site — non-acid soil	S:D	Cut back old stems — after flowering	Buy	Fragrant blooms in May and early June
TAMARIX	Tamarisk	Sunny site — well-drained soil	S:D	Cut back summer types — March	Cuttings — autumn	Spring varieties pale pink — summer ones deep pink or red
ULEX	Gorse	Sunny site — ordinary soil	S:E	Trim back — May	Cuttings — summer	Yellow flowers (April–May) on spiny stems. Poor on fertile sites
VIBURNUM	Viburnum	Sunny site — humus-rich soil	S: D or E	Not necessary	Cuttings — summer	Many varieties — year-round colour is possible by growing several types
VINCA	Periwinkle	Sun or shade — well-drained soil	S:E	Not necessary	Plant rooted suckers	An excellent ground cover. White or blue flowers in May-September
WEIGELA	Weigela	Sun or light shade — ordinary soil	S:D	Cut back shoots with faded blooms	Cuttings — summer	An old favourite — arching stems bear pink or red flowers in May and June
WISTERIA	Wistaria	Sunny site — fertile soil	C:D	Cut back current side growths — July	Layer stems — summer	Several types available — W. sinensis is the popular one

S: = shrub   T: = tree   C: = climber   D = deciduous   E = evergreen

Conifers

Latin name	Common name	Notes	Species & Varieties			
			Latin name	Ultimate height	Height after 10 years	Notes
ABIES	Silver Fir	Most firs are giants — choose with care	A. balsamea Hudsonia	DWARF	1 ft	Ideal for rock gardens
			A. koreana	MEDIUM	6 ft	Dark green foliage
ARAUCARIA	Monkey Puzzle	Once very popular — reaches 70 ft in time	A. araucana	TALL	5 ft	Branches like curved ropes
CEDRUS	Cedar	A tree for parkland rather than a suburban garden	C. atlantica Glauca	TALL	10 ft	Very popular — blue-green
			C. deodara	TALL	10 ft	Drooping growth habit
			C. libani	TALL	10 ft	Flat-topped with age
CHAMAECYPARIS	False Cypress	The most popular evergreen trees in Britain. Scores of varieties are available, ranging from rockery dwarfs to stately trees	C. lawsoniana Allumii	MEDIUM	6 ft	Conical — blue-grey foliage
			C. l. Ellwoodii	DWARF	5 ft	Very popular — grey-green
			C. l. Ellwood's Gold	DWARF	4 ft	Branchlet tips golden-yellow
			C. l. Minima Aurea	DWARF	1 ft	Compact pyramid — bright yellow
			C. l. Minima Glauca	DWARF	1 ft	Rounded — sea green foliage
			C. obtusa Nana Gracilis	DWARF	2 ft	Rounded sprays — dark foliage
			C. pisifera Boulevard	DWARF	3 ft	Silver-blue feathery sprays
CRYPTOMERIA	Japanese Cedar	Slow-growing — needs acid soil	C. japonica Elegans	MEDIUM	6 ft	Brown-green feathery sprays
CUPRESSO-CYPARIS	Leyland Cypress	The fastest growing conifer in Britain	C. leylandii	TALL	30 ft	Most popular conifer hedge
			C. l. Castlewellan	TALL	30 ft	Yellow foliage in spring
CUPRESSUS	Cypress	More difficult than Chamaecyparis	C. arizonica	MEDIUM	7 ft	Conical — blue-grey foliage
			C. macrocarpa Goldcrest	MEDIUM	8 ft	Conical — golden foliage
GINKGO	Maidenhair Tree	Unusual — leaves are wide and deciduous	G. biloba	TALL	10 ft	Pale green fan-like foliage
JUNIPERUS	Juniper	Most popular Junipers are either dwarfs or spreading ground covers. All are easy to grow, withstanding cold and poor soil conditions	J. chinensis	DWARF	5 ft	Conical — blue-green foliage
			J. communis Compressa	DWARF	1 ft	Columnar — grey-green foliage
			J. c. Depressa Aurea	DWARF	1 ft	Spreading — golden foliage
			J. horizontalis Glauca	PROSTRATE	1 ft	9 ft wide blue carpet
			J. media Pfitzerana	DWARF	4 ft	Popular — wide-spreading
			J. squamata Meyeri	DWARF	4 ft	Erect — blue-grey foliage
			J. virginiana Skyrocket	MEDIUM	6 ft	Blue-grey narrow column
LARIX	Larch	Deciduous — too tall for average garden	L. decidua	TALL	15 ft	Needs space and acid soil
METASEQUOIA	Dawn Redwood	Deciduous — discovered in 1941	M. glyptostroboides	TALL	15 ft	Orange foliage in autumn
PICEA	Spruce	Most (but not all) Piceas look like Christmas Trees. Dislike dry and chalky soils	P. albertiana Conica	DWARF	2 ft	Popular rockery conifer
			P. breweriana	TALL	5 ft	Excellent weeping conifer
			P. omorika	TALL	10 ft	Best Christmas Tree
			P. pungens Koster	MEDIUM	6 ft	Most popular Blue Spruce
PINUS	Pine	Pines are usually too tall for the average garden, but dwarf varieties are available	P. mugo Gnom	DWARF	2 ft	Globular rockery Pine
			P. nigra	TALL	10 ft	Dark green foliage
			P. strobus Nana	DWARF	2 ft	Spreading — silvery foliage
			P. sylvestris	TALL	12 ft	Familiar Scots Pine
TAXODIUM	Swamp Cypress	Deciduous — thrives in swampy soil	T. distichum	TALL	15 ft	Large tree — ferny foliage
TAXUS	Yew	Yews are generally slow-growing. Suitable for shade	T. baccata	MEDIUM	6 ft	Dark green tree or hedge
			T. b. Fastigiata	MEDIUM	5 ft	Columnar Irish Yew
			T. b. Semperaurea	DWARF	2 ft	Spreading — golden foliage
THUJA	Arbor-vitae	Similar to the much more popular Chamaecyparis. Many make excellent hedges	T. occidentalis Rheingold	DWARF	3 ft	Conical — bronzy foliage
			T. orientalis Aurea Nana	DWARF	2 ft	Globular — golden foliage
			T. o. Rosedalis	DWARF	2 ft	Globular — purple in autumn
			T. plicata	TALL	16 ft	Pyramid — specimen tree
TSUGA	Hemlock	Most types too tall for gardens	T. canadensis Pendula	DWARF	2 ft	Spreading — weeping branches

PROSTRATE = under 1½ ft   DWARF = 1½–15 ft   MEDIUM = 15–50 ft   TALL = over 50 ft

CHAPTER 4
Garden Friendly —
DOING THE WORK

WATERING

Soil which bears an average crop of plants loses about 4½ gallons of water per sq. yard every week during the summer months — this is equivalent to 1 in. of rain or applied water. In spring and autumn the loss is 2 gallons per week — ½ in. of rain or tap water.

This water has to come from the soil's reserves. If there is no rain and you have not watered the ground then drying out occurs. A prolonged dry spell can result in serious losses, especially in the high risk areas listed below. But even deep-rooted established plants such as Roses can suffer — trials have shown that growth is impaired and the flowering season is shortened if these plants are not watered during a dry summer.

Don't wait until the dry days of summer before you begin your battle against water shortage. Follow the 6 step plan set out below.

AREAS MOST AT RISK

- Bedding plants for 4–6 weeks after planting
- Plants growing in tubs
- Herbaceous perennials for the first year after planting
- Shrubs and trees for the first 2 years after planting

- Plants growing within 2 ft of the house
- Plants growing in light soil
- Tomatoes, Cucumbers, Onions, Marrows, Beans & Celery
- Shallow-rooted plants. Some are large — e.g Silver Birch

Drought

VISUAL EFFECTS

- First, foliage looks dull
- Next, leaf edges start to roll
- Next, wilting takes place. Browning occurs progressively from the leaf tips
- Finally, flowering stops — leaves fall — the plant dies

The 6 STEP plan to avoid dry weather problems

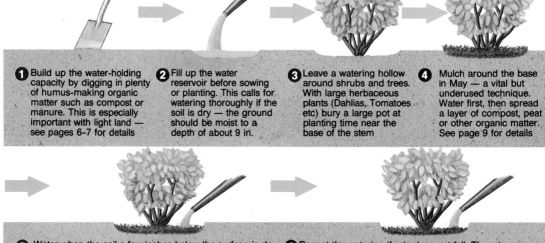

1 Build up the water-holding capacity by digging in plenty of humus-making organic matter such as compost or manure. This is especially important with light land — see pages 6–7 for details

2 Fill up the water reservoir before sowing or planting. This calls for watering thoroughly if the soil is dry — the ground should be moist to a depth of about 9 in.

3 Leave a watering hollow around shrubs and trees. With large herbaceous plants (Dahlias, Tomatoes etc) bury a large pot at planting time near the base of the stem

4 Mulch around the base in May — a vital but underused technique. Water first, then spread a layer of compost, peat or other organic matter. See page 9 for details

5 Water when the soil a few inches below the surface is dry and the foliage is dull. Never apply a small amount every few days. Use 1–4 gallons to fill the watering hollow or pot — see step 3 above. Hold the watering can spout or hose nozzle close to the ground and water slowly. Use 2–4 gallons per sq. yd when watering overall

6 Repeat the watering if rain does not fall. There is no easy way to determine the right time for this repeat watering — dig down with a trowel and examine the soil at 3–4 in. below the surface. If it is dry, then water. As a general rule watering is required every 7 days during a period of drought in summer

GROWING IN BEDS

Our present custom of growing annual flowers in flat beds and sowing vegetables in long rows began well over a hundred years ago. These two concepts have become accepted as basic parts of the gardening scene, but 'new' ideas concerning the construction and maintenance of beds appeared during the 1980s — ideas which were actually in use hundreds of years ago. There is no doubt that the raised bed for flowers and the permanent bed for vegetables will become widely used during the 1990s — they are both Bio Friendly.

Raised beds for ornamentals

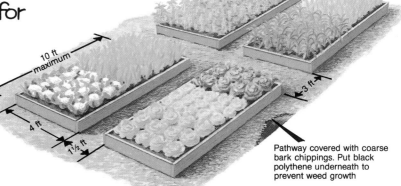

Walls of stone, brick, concrete blocks, peat blocks, railway sleepers etc

Wall face can be planted if dry walling (no mortar between stones) or peat blocks are used. Plant as you go when building the wall

The walls must be firm, especially if a large amount of soil is to be retained. Sink part of the bottom course of walling material into the ground and stagger rectangular blocks as shown above. Make sure that the walling material is attractive in its own right or plan to cover it with trailing plants.

For a single retaining wall against a bank it is necessary to create a satisfactory foundation and to tilt the wall slightly inwards against the soil.

Break up the soil at the bottom of the bed. Add a layer of broken bricks or rubble and cover with peat, old growing bag compost or reversed turves. Add the soil mixture — leave to settle for a couple of weeks before planting.

USES

Growing acid-loving plants You can grow Azaleas, Camellias etc in chalky soil by filling a raised bed with a mixture of soil and sphagnum peat

Growing alpine plants The *only* way to grow choice and small alpines in most gardens. Drainage is improved, plants are raised closer to eye level and a rockery planting mix can be used — 2 parts soil, 1 part peat and 1 part grit

Improving drainage Plant roots can be kept away from the high water table in badly-drained soil

Helping elderly or disabled gardeners The removal of the need to bend to ground level makes planting and maintenance easier

Improving display Small plants can be lost from view when grown in a flat bed

Permanent beds for vegetables

Flat beds The easiest type to create, but you do need fertile and free-draining soil. Simply turn over the soil and work in a 1 in. layer of organic matter

Deep beds Use if drainage is not very good or the soil has a poor structure. Double dig — see pages 12–13 of The Garden Expert. Work organic matter into the top spit of soil as well as into the ground below

Raised beds Use if drainage is poor and waterlogging is a problem. Create retaining walls — see section above for details. Flat wooden boards can be used — attach firmly to wooden corner posts. Raised beds should be at least 4 in. high — fork over bottom before filling with a mixture of 2 part soil/1 part organic matter

10 ft maximum

4 ft

1½ ft

3 ft

Pathway covered with coarse bark chippings. Put black polythene underneath to prevent weed growth

Growing vegetables in permanent beds rather than in rows has several distinct advantages. General maintenance is much easier — closely-planted vegetables smother most weeds and there are no muddy walkways between rows. Yields are higher — plants are closely set in blocks so that the plants just touch neighbouring ones when mature. Finally, heavy digging is no longer necessary — for many this is a no-dig way of growing.

Construct beds to run N–S if possible. Always add organic matter and leave the soil to settle for at least a couple of weeks before planting or sowing. See page 20 for sowing distances. Plant short rows in the bed every 1–3 weeks to avoid gluts.

Each autumn or early winter add a layer of organic matter to the surface and work in. You should not need to dig for several years, or perhaps not at all. Practice crop rotation — see page 19.

PLANTING IN POTS, TRAYS & BAGS

The Standard Pot

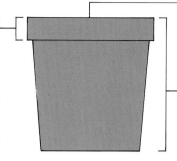

Watering Space
This is the recommended distance from the compost level to the top of the pot.

Pot Size	Watering Space
2½–5 in.	½ in.
5½–7½ in.	¾ in.
8–9 in.	1 in.
10–12 in.	1½ in.
15 in.	2 in.

Diameter inside rim
This is the size of the pot — a 5 in. pot has a 5 in. diameter inside rim.

Height
The height of the pot is approximately the same as the diameter.

CLAY POT

Advantages:
- Heavy; much less liable to topple over.
- Waterlogging is less likely because of porous nature.
- Traditional 'natural' appearance — no chance of colour clashes.
- Damaging salts are leached away from the compost.

Standard Pots
see panel above for details

Half Pots
use for Bulbs, Azalea, Bromeliads, Begonia semperflorens and Saintpaulia

PLASTIC POT

Advantages:
- Lightweight; much less liable to break if dropped.
- Watering is needed less often.
- Decorative and colourful forms available.
- No crocking needed; easy to clean.

Seed Pans
for drawback see seed tray section below

PEAT POT

Peat pots are made from compressed peat — most are impregnated with fertilizer. The pot is bio-degradable and is planted into the soil or compost. Expensive if a large number of plants are grown. Square version is available.

FELT POT

Felt pots are made from felt sheeting impregnated with bitumen. These black pots are available in the 2¼–3½ in. range. They do not get soggy when wet and can be planted directly into the soil. The pot is bio-degradable.

PEAT PELLET

Peat pellets are made from dried and compressed peat. They expand when soaked in water — the plastic netting around them provides support. The pot is planted directly into the soil, so no root disturbance takes place.

POLYTHENE SLEEVE POT

Polythene sleeve pots are made from black plastic sheeting. They are inexpensive and easily stored but not easily filled with compost. These pots are usually thrown away but can be re-used if not torn.

SEED TRAY

Seed trays are made from plastic or wood — the standard one is 14 in. x 8½ in. x 2 in. Seeds germinate well in these inexpensive and re-usable containers — the trouble is root disturbance at pricking out time. Not suitable for Lettuce or large seeds.

CELLULAR SEED TRAY

The polystyrene tray has a number of cells which are filled with compost and sown with 1–3 seeds. At transplanting time a pusher plate is used to remove the blocks — these are planted into the soil.

The 4 stages of Potting

1 **PRICKING OUT**

This is carried out when a seedling is ready to be transferred from a seed tray or pan into its first pot — usually a 2½ or 3 in. clay or plastic pot.

or

This is carried out when a rooted cutting is ready to be transferred into its first pot — usually a 2½ or 3 in. clay or plastic pot.

POTTING UP

2 **POTTING ON**

This is carried out when the roots have filled the pot and the plant is starting to become pot-bound. Check by removing the pot in the way shown below. If it is pot-bound there will be a mass of roots on the outside and not much soil is visible. Potting on into a larger pot is now necessary to encourage the plant to develop further.

A suitable sequence of pot sizes is 3 in. → 5 in. → 7 in. → 10 in. Never miss out a stage in this sequence, but stop when the desired plant size is reached. Scrub out old pots — soak clay ones overnight.

Water the plant. One hour later remove it from the pot as shown above. If difficult to dislodge, knock pot on the edge of a table and run a knife around the rootball. Remove old crocks. Tease out matted roots.

Cover drainage hole of a clay pot with crocks. Add a layer of potting compost. Place the plant on top of layer — gradually fill surrounding space with damp potting compost. Firm compost with your thumbs.

Tap pot several times on table — leave ¾–1 in. watering space. Water carefully. Keep in the shade for a week — mist the leaves daily. Then place the plant in its growing quarters and treat normally.

3 **RE-POTTING**

This is carried out when the plant and/or pot has reached the desired or maximum size. Remove the plant as above and tease some of the old compost away from the rootball. Trim away some of the root tips, but do not reduce the rootball size by more than 20 per cent. Pot on as described above, using the same size of pot. Wash the old container thoroughly if it is to be re-used.

4 **TOP-DRESSING**

This is carried out when you do not wish to or are unable to re-pot. This occurs with large plants which are too heavy to lift, trained specimens and plants which are tied to supports. In this case the pot should be top-dressed each spring by carefully removing the top 1 in. of compost — 2 in. for large pots. This removed material is discarded and replaced with fresh Bio Friendly Universal Compost.

Growing Bags

Growing bags have revolutionised the growing of Tomatoes, Cucumbers, Lettuce etc under glass. They are also suitable for brightening up the patio with a display of bedding plants — when used for floral display it is a good idea to plant trailers around the edge to hide the polythene. The great advantage with disease-prone crops such as Melons, Tomatoes and so on is the absence of plant-harming fungi as well as freedom from underground pests. The standard bag is 39 in. long and weighs about 35 lb. Carrying them can be a strain for the elderly or infirm — half bags (Bio Bolsters) are available. Excellent fruit, vegetables and bedding plants can be grown this way, but only if you learn the rules for watering. These are different to the technique with pots and border soil. Waterlogging is a danger, so follow the instructions carefully.

Composts

Modern composts are based on peat and have several advantages over soil composts. They are light and easy to handle, but the main blessing is reliability — good quality loam is scarce these days. Nutrients have to be incorporated with the base to ensure that the plants have sufficient food for at least a couple of months before fertilizer is required. Bio Friendly Universal Compost contains all the major plant foods — nitrogen, phosphorus and potash. These elements plus magnesium and calcium are sourced entirely from organics and minerals. Potting is the main use, but it is equally suitable for raising seeds, taking cuttings and for filling window boxes and hanging baskets.

Re-using Growing Bags

Used bags may contain diseases and pests, and the nutrient balance will undoubtedly be different than it was when you bought them. It is still quite practical to re-use a growing bag if you follow a few simple rules. Remove the old plants — rootballs as well as stems. Add some fresh compost or peat and mix in thoroughly. Next, you *must* change the crop. You can grow Tomatoes after Cucumbers and vice versa, but it is preferable to pick less demanding plants. Good candidates are Spring Onions, Strawberries, Herbs, Bulbs, French Beans, Radishes, Lettuces and bedding plants.

PLANTING

You will never finish stocking your garden as long as you remain a gardener. The quickest way to obtain instant colour and greenery is to use **container-grown plants** — root disturbance is avoided. A container-grown plant will have been raised as a seedling, cutting or grafted rootstock and then potted on until housed in a whalehide, plastic or metal container. Pot-grown plants are miniature versions.

There are times when you will have to rely on **lifted plants** such as perennials dug up at the nursery, bedding plants grown in trays or vegetables moved from a nursery bed. Evergreens are often sold as balled plants — the soil ball is tightly wrapped with netting or polythene sheeting after lifting.

Bare-rooted plants are dug up at the nursery and transported without soil — once all Roses were bought this way. Damp material such as peat is packed around the roots to prevent drying out. Bare-rooted plants are less expensive than their container-grown counterparts but it is not true that they are always more difficult to establish. Some shrubs actually root more easily.

Bio Friendly Humus

Bio Friendly Humus is made by setting out organic matter, seaweed and other nutrients in large stacks. After a long period of intense bacterial digestion a fully-composted soil improver rich in humus is formed. This material cannot scorch delicate plant roots. The root-promoting action of Bio Friendly Humus is due to the seaweed and other organic extracts added before processing and the colloids which are formed during the digestion process.

The main use of Bio Friendly Humus is at planting time — a 1 in. layer is spread at the bottom of the hole before planting trees, shrubs, soft and tree fruit etc. It is also used for spreading along seed drills, mulching and placing under bedding plants.

Planting Mixture

With bare-rooted plants you should use a planting mixture rather than ordinary soil when filling the planting hole. This is not essential, but it is recommended if your soil is either heavy or light. Using a planting mixture instead of ordinary soil is even more important with container-grown plants — roots hate to move from the peat-rich compost of the container into a mineral garden soil which is practically devoid of organic matter.

Make up the planting mixture in a wheelbarrow on a day when the soil is reasonably dry — 1 part topsoil, 1 part moist peat and 3 handfuls of Bone Meal per barrowload. Keep this mixture in a shed or garage until you are ready to start planting.

Lifted Plants

Choose a day when the soil is moist. Squeeze a handful of the soil — it should be wet enough to form a ball and yet dry enough to shatter when dropped on a hard surface.

Prepare plants for the move. Always water plants prior to lifting — dry soil would fall away from the roots. Do all you can to keep the soil ball intact.

Plant properly. For small plants, fill around the soil ball with loose soil and firm with the fingers or the trowel handle. With larger plants, fine soil should be added, each layer being gently compressed with the fists until the hole is full. Stake trees at planting time. Handle non-woody plants by the soil ball or the leaves — never by the stem. Water in after planting.

Use the right tool. Use a spade for planting trees, shrubs and mature perennials. A trowel is the right tool for small plants and a dibber (short pointed stick) for 'greens'.

Plant at the right depth. Set all bedding plants, seedlings and rooted cuttings so that the top of the soil ball is just below ground level. With lifted mature plants use the old soil mark on the stems as your guide.

Dig the hole to fit the roots. The hole should be much wider than it is deep — the roots at the base and at the side should never have to be bent to fit into the hole.

Bare-rooted Plants

GOOD SIGNS: Root system well developed — spreading in all directions

BAD SIGNS: Shrivelled stems, white roots growing in the peat, open leaf buds

Planting time is the dormant season between autumn and spring — choose mid October–late November if you can, but delay planting until March if the soil is heavy and wet. Cut off leaves, dead flowers, weak stems and damaged roots. If the stem is shrivelled plunge the roots in a bucket of water for 2 hours before planting

(2) The old soil mark should be level with the soil surface — set a board across the top of the hole to ensure correct planting depth

(4) Add more planting mixture until the hole is full. Firm by pressing with the fists or gentle treading — on no account tread heavily. Loosen the surface once the hole has been filled

(3) Work a couple of trowelfuls of the planting mixture around the roots. Shake the plant gently up and down — add a little more planting mixture. Firm this around the roots with the fists — do not press too hard. Half-fill the hole with more planting mixture and firm it down

(1) The hole should be wide enough to allow the roots to be spread evenly. Put a layer of Bio Friendly Humus at the bottom of the hole — important if soil condition is poor

Container-grown Plants

GOOD SIGNS: Small weeds on surface, small roots peeping through container

BAD SIGNS: Wilted or diseased leaves, split container, thick root growing through base

A large container-grown plant should *not* have been lifted from the open ground and its roots and surrounding soil stuffed into the container prior to sale. The test is to pull the plant gently and see if the soil ball comes up easily. If it does, the plant should be rejected. Planting can take place at any time of the year, but the soil must be neither frozen nor waterlogged

(2) Water the container thoroughly. Cut down the side of the container when it is stood in the hole. Remove the cover and its base very carefully — do not disturb the soil ball

(4) After planting there should be a shallow water-holding basin

(3) Examine the exposed surface — cut away circling or tangled roots but do not break up the soil ball. Fill the space between the soil ball and the sides of the hole with planting mixture. Firm down the planting mixture with your hands

(1) The hole should be deep enough to ensure that the top of the soil ball will be about 1 in. below the soil surface after planting. The hole should be wide enough for the soil ball to be surrounded by a 3–4 in. layer of planting mixture. Put a 1 in. layer of Bio Friendly Humus or planting mixture at the bottom of the hole

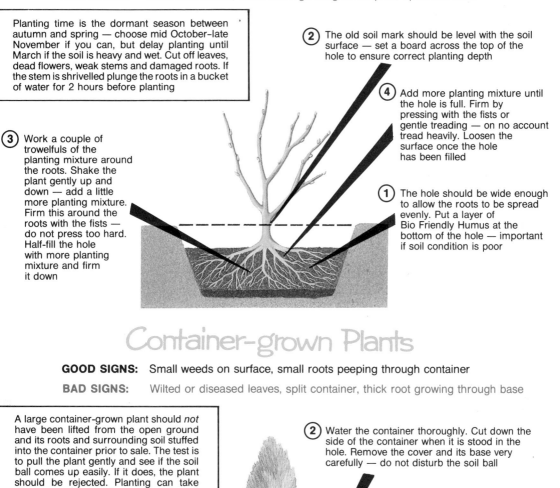

INCREASING YOUR STOCK

Sowing seed is undoubtedly the easiest way to raise a large number of plants for the garden. It is the standard technique for raising annual flowers —hardy types are sown outdoors in March and April when the soil is warm enough for germination and dry enough to allow you to make a seed bed. Most vegetables are also sown outdoors, but you cannot generalise about the correct time to sow — see page 19 for the basic rules for sowing outdoors.

Half-hardy annuals can be sown outdoors when the danger of frost is past, but it is better to sow them under glass, using the technique shown below. Some perennials can be raised successfully from seed, but it is more usual to use a vegetative (non-seed) method of propagation to ensure that the new plants will be true to type. Clumps of border perennials and clusters of bulbs can be divided up at re-planting time. When splitting border plants (see illustration), use the divisions from the outer part of the clump — discard the old centre. The standard method for increasing the stock of perennials and shrubs is to take cuttings — see page 35.

Some Roses such as vigorous Floribundas can be successfully propagated from cuttings, but most Rose varieties and all fruit trees are grafted on to specially selected rootstocks. Leave this to the professional and buy the new plants you need from the garden centre or other supplier.

Sowing Seeds

1 **SEED** You must start with good quality seed. Buy from a reputable supplier and don't open the packet until you are ready to sow. Store unused seed in a screw-top jar — put it in a cool and dark place. Do not store opened packets of pelleted or dressed seed. Saving and sowing seed from your own plants often gives disappointing results — do not save seed from F_1 hybrids.

2 **CONTAINER** Use a seed tray, pan or ordinary flower pot. Drainage holes or cracks are necessary. Wash used containers thoroughly before filling — soak clay pots overnight.

3 **COMPOST** A peat-based seed compost provides an ideal medium for germination — sterile, light and consistent. Fill the container with Bio Friendly Universal Compost. Firm lightly with a piece of board. Sprinkle the compost with water the day before seed sowing — it should be moist (not wet) when you sow the seeds. Scatter them thinly and cover with a thin layer of compost — small seeds should not be covered. Firm lightly with a board.

4 **COVER** Put brown paper over the tray or pot and place a sheet of glass over it. Condensation is absorbed by the paper and so does not drip on to the compost below. Change the paper if necessary.

5 **WARMTH** Some garden seeds will germinate quite happily at 50°F or less, but some plants such as Tomatoes require 60°-70°F for satisfactory germination. You cannot expect to maintain such temperatures in an unheated room in spring, so you have two choices. A heated propagator is the more satisfactory answer, but if one is not available you can place the pot or tray on the windowsill of a centrally-heated room which is kept above the recommended minimum temperature.

6 **LIGHT** As soon as the seedlings break through the surface, remove the paper and prop up the sheet of glass. After a few days the glass should be removed and the container moved to a bright but sunless spot. Keep the compost moist but not wet.

7 **PRICK OUT** As soon as the first set of true leaves has opened the seedlings should be pricked out into trays, pans or small pots filled with Universal Compost. Handle the plants by the seed leaves — not the stems. The seedlings should be set about 1½ in. apart. Keep the container in the shade for a day or two after pricking out.

8 **HARDEN OFF** When the seedlings have recovered from the pricking out move, they must be hardened off to prepare them for the life outdoors. Increase the ventilation and move the container to a cool room or to a cold frame. Then move outdoors during daylight hours; finally leaving them outdoors all the time for about 7 days before planting out.

Correct
stage for
pricking out

Taking Cuttings

A cutting is a small piece removed from a plant which with proper treatment can be induced to form roots and then grow into a specimen which is identical to the parent plant. You cannot guess the best type of cutting to take nor the best time to propagate it — consult The Flower Expert and The Tree & Shrub Expert. There are, however, a few general rules. Plant the cutting as soon as possible after severing it from the parent plant and make sure that the compost is in close contact with the inserted part. Do not keep pulling at the cutting to see if it has rooted — the appearance of new growth is the best guide.

SOFTWOOD & SEMI-RIPE CUTTINGS

Softwood cuttings are green at the tip and base, and are taken from early spring to midsummer. Many hardy perennials and some small shrubs are propagated in this way. Basal cuttings are shoots formed at the base of the plant and pulled away for use as softwood cuttings in spring. **Semi-ripe cuttings** are green at the top and partly woody at the base — they are usually heel cuttings (see below). Midsummer to early autumn is the usual time and most shrubs, climbers and conifers are propagated by this method.

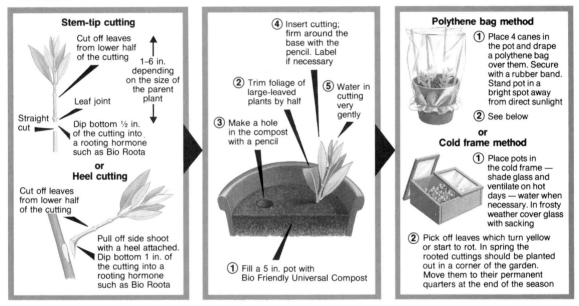

Stem-tip cutting

Cut off leaves from lower half of the cutting

1–6 in. depending on the size of the parent plant

Leaf joint

Straight cut

Dip bottom ½ in. of the cutting into a rooting hormone such as Bio Roota

or
Heel cutting

Cut off leaves from lower half of the cutting

Pull off side shoot with a heel attached. Dip bottom 1 in. of the cutting into a rooting hormone such as Bio Roota

④ Insert cutting; firm around the base with the pencil. Label if necessary

② Trim foliage of large-leaved plants by half

③ Make a hole in the compost with a pencil

⑤ Water in cutting very gently

① Fill a 5 in. pot with Bio Friendly Universal Compost

Polythene bag method

① Place 4 canes in the pot and drape a polythene bag over them. Secure with a rubber band. Stand pot in a bright spot away from direct sunlight

② See below

or
Cold frame method

① Place pots in the cold frame — shade glass and ventilate on hot days — water when necessary. In frosty weather cover glass with sacking

② Pick off leaves which turn yellow or start to rot. In spring the rooted cuttings should be planted out in a corner of the garden. Move them to their permanent quarters at the end of the season

HARDWOOD CUTTINGS

A large variety of trees, shrubs, Roses and soft fruit can be propagated in this way. The usual time is late autumn. Choose a well-ripened shoot of this year's growth.

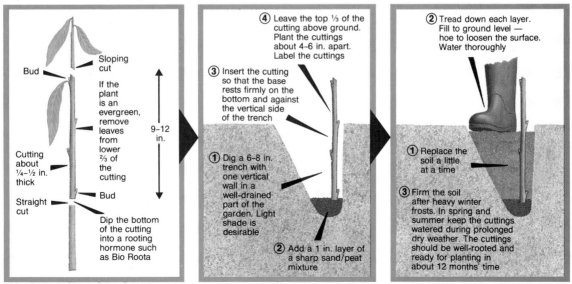

Bud

Sloping cut

If the plant is an evergreen, remove leaves from lower ⅔ of the cutting

9–12 in.

Cutting about ¼–½ in. thick

Bud

Straight cut

Dip the bottom of the cutting into a rooting hormone such as Bio Roota

④ Leave the top ⅓ of the cutting above ground. Plant the cuttings about 4–6 in. apart. Label the cuttings

③ Insert the cutting so that the base rests firmly on the bottom and against the vertical side of the trench

① Dig a 6–8 in. trench with one vertical wall in a well-drained part of the garden. Light shade is desirable

② Add a 1 in. layer of a sharp sand/peat mixture

② Tread down each layer. Fill to ground level — hoe to loosen the surface. Water thoroughly

① Replace the soil a little at a time

③ Firm the soil after heavy winter frosts. In spring and summer keep the cuttings watered during prolonged dry weather. The cuttings should be well-rooted and ready for planting in about 12 months' time

FEEDING

All soils have a stock of the elements which serve as plant nutrients. When the ground is cultivated and plants grown in it, these elements essential to plant growth start to disappear.

We need to replenish the ones used in large amounts — every gardening expert agrees that nitrogen, phosphorus and potassium must be added to the soil at regular intervals. A proportion is provided by humus makers (see pages 6–7), but we must rely on fertilizers as the main source of supply. *A fertilizer is a material which provides appreciable quantities of one or more of the major plant nutrients without adding significantly to the humus content of the soil.*

There are three basic types of fertilizer — organic, natural and chemical. The basic differences are outlined on the right, and many proprietary brands of fertilizer are a mixture of two or all three types. Organics break down in the same way as chemicals in the soil and plant roots take up the same simple salts from both types. But the organic/natural supporters believe there *are* differences — the organic and natural plant foods tend to stay in the soil longer and the nitrate release is slower. The Bio Friendly approach uses this view as its base.

ORGANIC FERTILIZERS

These materials are of animal or vegetable origin. They are generally slow-acting, providing plants with a steady supply of food over a long period. Not likely to scorch leaves. Nitrogen is released by bacterial activity, so speed of action depends on soil conditions.

NATURAL FERTILIZERS

These materials are obtained from neither plants nor animals — they are minerals mined from the earth. Some of them (gypsum, dolomite limestone and chalk) provide calcium and are described on page 10. The others provide nitrogen, phosphorus and/or potash — they may be quick- or slow-acting.

CHEMICAL FERTILIZERS

These are manufactured materials and have earned the titles of 'synthetic' or 'artificial' fertilizers. They are generally quick-acting, providing plants with a boost when used as a top-dressing. Popular examples include sulphate of ammonia and superphosphate of lime.

The Bio Friendly Feeding Plan

1 Add Bone Meal to the soil before planting permanent or semi-permanent plants such as Roses, trees and shrubs

2 Incorporate Bio Friendly Plant Food into the soil when preparing the ground for flowers and vegetables. Apply an annual dressing in spring around Roses, border plants, trees and shrubs. Sprinkle a small handful per sq. yard over the lawn if it looks jaded in spring or early summer

3 Repeat the treatment in summer if further feeding is obviously necessary. Or you can put on a dressing of Leaf Maker if nitrogen is needed or Flower Maker if potash is required. See the table below for guidance

4 Pot plants require a liquid fertilizer. Use Bio Plant Food for greenhouse plants and Baby Bio for house plants

Plant Nutrients

PLANT NUTRIENT	PLANTS MOST IN NEED	SOILS MOST IN NEED	SIGNS OF SHORTAGE
NITROGEN (N) the LEAF MAKER	Grass • Vegetables grown for their leaves • Root-bound plants	Sandy soils • Rainy areas	Stunted growth • Small, pale green leaves • Weak stems
PHOSPHATES (P_2O_5) the ROOT MAKER	Young plants • Root vegetables • Fruit and seed crops	Sandy soils	Stunted growth • Small leaves with a purplish tinge • Low fruit yield
POTASH (K_2O) the FLOWER and FRUIT MAKER	Fruit • Flowers • Potatoes	Sandy soils	Brown leaf edges • Low fruit yield — fruit and flowers poorly coloured • Low disease resistance
MAGNESIUM (Mg)	Roses • Tomatoes	Sandy soils • Peaty soils • K_2O-rich soils	Yellow or brown patches between the veins of older leaves • Young leaves may fall
IRON (Fe) MANGANESE (Mn)	Rhododendrons • Azaleas • Camellias	Chalky soils	Yellowing of young leaves
OTHERS (Sulphur, Calcium, Boron, Zinc, Copper, Molybdenum)	Various	Various	Various — the use of humus makers, fertilizers and liming materials generally supplies sufficient amounts

Fertilizer Notes

- Do not sprinkle fertilizer along seed drills.
- Do not feed plants with powder fertilizers right up to the stems. The feeding roots are some distance away from this region. Keep solid fertilizers off leaves and flowers. Wash off with water if these parts are accidentally treated.

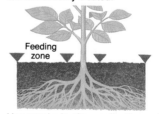

Feeding zone

- Hoe or rake in after application and water if rain seems unlikely.
- If the application rate is 1 oz or less per sq. yard, mix the fertilizer with sand to improve the evenness of the cover obtained.
- Make sure that you use the amount recommended on the package. Double the amount does not give twice the benefit — it can in fact lead to unbalanced growth.
- Do not store fertilizer bags or cartons in a damp place. Always close the top after use and keep the packages off the floor.

ORGANIC & NATURAL FERTILIZERS

Bio Friendly Plant Food is composed entirely of organic and natural fertilizers — there are no manufactured chemicals or inactive fillers such as sand or peat.

Contains:

FISH MEAL   SEAWEED MEAL
+
BLOOD MEAL   ROCK POTASH
+
BONE FLOUR   GYPSUM

1 large handful per sq. yd is raked in before sowing or planting. In spring it is spread at the rate of 1 handful per sq. yd around growing plants — a repeat treatment can be applied in summer. The rate for trees and shrubs is 1 large handful around each plant.

Bio Friendly Bone Meal is used at 2–4 oz per sq. yd during general soil preparation in autumn or early spring. At planting time it is one of the ingredients of the planting mixture to fill the hole — see page 32 for the formula.

It is also used for feeding established trees, bushes, borders etc at the rate of 2–4 oz per sq. yd in spring — the fertilizer is worked into the top inch or two.

Bone Meal has been used for generations as a slow release source of nitrogen and phosphate. The Bio Friendly grade has been heat-treated for maximum safety.

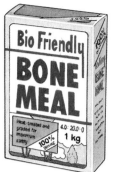

Fertilizer	Nitrogen % N	Phosphates % P_2O_5	Potash % K_2O	Speed of Action	Application rate per sq. yd	Notes
BIO FRIENDLY PLANT FOOD	7	5	5	FQ	2–4 oz	Apply at soil preparation or planting time — use around growing plants in spring/summer
BLOOD MEAL	12	trace	trace	FQ	1–2 oz	Use as a top-dressing around growing plants in spring/summer. Quick-acting under glass
BONE FLOUR	1	20–28	0	FQ	2–4 oz	Lower in nitrogen and dustier than Bone Meal, but it acts more quickly
BONE MEAL	4	20	0	S	2–4 oz	Apply at soil preparation or planting time. Use a 'heat-treated' grade for safety
CHILEAN POTASH NITRATE	15	0	10	Q	1–2 oz	Use as a quick-acting top-dressing in spring/early summer — not generally available
FISH MEAL	6–10	6–12	1–3	S–FQ	2–4 oz	Apply at soil preparation or planting time in winter or spring. Potash is usually very low
HOOF & HORN MEAL	14	2	0	S–FQ	2–4 oz	A good source of organic nitrogen — slower than Blood Meal. Apply in spring or early summer
POULTRY MANURE (DRIED)	4	3	2	S–FQ	2–8 oz	High rate is used at soil preparation time — low rate is for around growing plants
ROCK PHOSPHATE	0	30	0	S	8 oz	Slow release source of phosphates — lasts for about 3 years. Good for acid soils
ROCK POTASH	0	0	10–12	S	8 oz	Slow release source of potash — lasts for about 3 years. Good for light soils
SEAWEED MEAL	3	trace	2	FQ	2 oz	Expensive, but a good source of trace elements. Use around plants in spring or summer
SHODDY	10	trace	trace	S	1 lb	Waste wool and/or cotton. A poor humus maker, but provides nitrogen over a period of years
SOOT	3–6	0	0	Q	4 oz	Must be weathered before use — no longer popular and not recommended as toxins are present
WOOD ASH	0	trace	5–10	Q	4–8 oz	Use young wood — keep in a dry place. Not recommended for chalky soils

S = slow
FQ = fairly quick
Q = quick

PRUNING

Pruning has a very simple meaning — the cutting away of unwanted growth from woody plants. But the purpose of pruning is less easy to understand, as there is nearly always more than one reason for carrying out this work:

- To remove poor quality wood, such as weak twigs, dead or diseased branches and damaged shoots.
- To shape the tree or shrub to your needs. This calls for the removal of healthy but unwanted wood — examples include the pruning of the central leader of a tree to produce an open-centred plant, the removal of a minor branch which is rubbing against a major one and the cutting back of branches which are blocking a pathway.
- To regulate both the quality and quantity of blossom and/or fruit production.

The craft of pruning is perhaps the most difficult lesson the gardener has to learn. There are a few general rules — use good tools and keep them sharp, cut out all dead and weak wood, pare off the edges of ragged cuts and keep hedges narrower at the top than at the base. But the timing and technique depend on the age and type of tree or shrub — consult the appropriate Expert book for details.

GARDEN SHEARS
are required for trimming hedges and tidying-up in the border. Buy a good pair and make sure they are properly set — keep them clean, dry and sharp

ARBREX
for painting all cuts over ½ in. diameter to protect the surface

TWO-BLADED SECATEURS
will cut cleanly for many years with proper care. The cut must be made at the centre of the blades — maximum diameter ½-¾ in.

PRUNING SAW
is useful if you have stems over ½ in. across to be cut

LONG-HANDLED PRUNER
for stems ½-1½ in. across — many gardeners prefer them to a pruning saw for dealing with thick stems. Essential for tall shrubs and trees

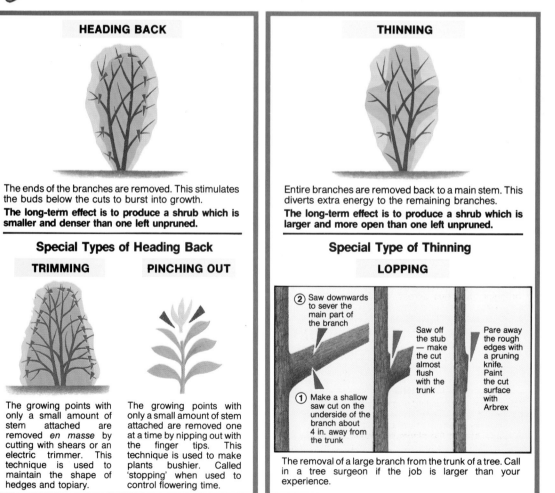

HEADING BACK

The ends of the branches are removed. This stimulates the buds below the cuts to burst into growth.

The long-term effect is to produce a shrub which is smaller and denser than one left unpruned.

Special Types of Heading Back

TRIMMING

The growing points with only a small amount of stem attached are removed *en masse* by cutting with shears or an electric trimmer. This technique is used to maintain the shape of hedges and topiary.

PINCHING OUT

The growing points with only a small amount of stem attached are removed one at a time by nipping out with the finger tips. This technique is used to make plants bushier. Called 'stopping' when used to control flowering time.

THINNING

Entire branches are removed back to a main stem. This diverts extra energy to the remaining branches.

The long-term effect is to produce a shrub which is larger and more open than one left unpruned.

Special Type of Thinning

LOPPING

② Saw downwards to sever the main part of the branch

① Make a shallow saw cut on the underside of the branch about 4 in. away from the trunk

Saw off the stub — make the cut almost flush with the trunk

Pare away the rough edges with a pruning knife. Paint the cut surface with Arbrex

The removal of a large branch from the trunk of a tree. Call in a tree surgeon if the job is larger than your experience.

OTHER JOBS

DEAD-HEADING

The removal of dead flowers has several advantages — it helps to keep the bed or border tidy, it prolongs the flowering season by preventing seed formation and in a few cases (e.g Lupin and Delphinium) it induces a second flush later in the season.

Use garden shears, secateurs, a sharp knife or finger tips depending on the type of plant. Be careful not to remove too much stem.

DISBUDDING

In general flower buds in the garden are allowed to develop and open naturally to provide the maximum display. For exhibitors, however, and others interested in the size of individual blooms, the flower-stems are disbudded. This calls for pinching out side buds as soon as they can be handled, leaving the central bud to develop into a large specimen to catch the eye of the judge or earn the envy of the neighbours.

FORKING

A garden fork is not really a digging tool, although it can sometimes be easier to dig a heavy soil with a fork rather than a spade. Forking is really a method of cultivation — lumps are broken down by hitting them with the tines and the surface roughly levelled by dragging the tines across the surface. Forking is also used around growing plants to break up the surface crust.

HEELING IN

Occasionally you will find that trees, shrubs, Roses or herbaceous perennials arrive before you are ready to plant them. If this delay is to be more than 10 days, heel in the plants by digging a shallow V-shaped trench and then spreading them as a single row against one side of the trench. Cover the roots and lower parts of the stems with soil and tread down.

PROTECTING IN WINTER

The snow and frost of an average winter usually do little or no harm to the trees and shrubs in the garden, but an abnormally severe winter can cause heavy losses. Newly-planted stock will benefit from some form of frost protection, especially if it is evergreen and known to be rather tender. You can either build a plastic screen (make sure that the bottom of the sheeting is pinned down to prevent draughts) or you can put a large plastic bag over the specimen on nights when a heavy frost is forecast.

Established plants are more resistant than newly-planted ones to frost, but they are more liable to damage by the other winter enemy — snow. If heavy snow is forecast it may be worth tying the branches of a choice evergreen with twine.

RAKING

The role of raking is to create a seed bed after the large lumps have been broken down by forking. Choose a day when the surface is dry but the soil below is moist. Work in long sweeps, drawing stones and rubbish towards you and breaking down lumps as you push away. After raking in this way, repeat at right angles. You must know when to stop — over-raking produces a tilth which caps with the first downpour.

STAKING

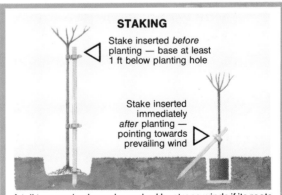

Stake inserted *before* planting — base at least 1 ft below planting hole

Stake inserted immediately *after* planting — pointing towards prevailing wind

A tall tree or shrub can be rocked by strong winds if its roots are not able to anchor it firmly in the ground. A newly-planted specimen does not have this anchorage, so it can be dislodged or blown over. Staking is the answer — it is a job to do at planting time and not after the damage has been done. Inspect ties regularly — adjust as stem thickens.

CHAPTER 5
Garden Friendly —
TACKLING THE PROBLEMS

The Bio Friendly gardener cannot call on the vast array of modern chemicals which are available to fight against pests and diseases. In most cases organic and natural products are relied upon, and these are sometimes not as effective or as wide-ranging as their sophisticated counterparts. It is therefore vital whenever possible for the Bio Friendly gardener to try to prevent problems from getting a hold in the garden.

PESTS are animals, varying in size from tiny eelworms to majestic deer, which attack plants. The general term 'insect' covers small pests — mites, slugs, woodlice and true insects.

DISEASES are plant troubles caused by living organisms which are transmitted from one plant to another. Fungal diseases are the most common. Others are caused by bacteria and viruses.

DISORDERS are plant troubles which have disease-like symptoms but which are not due to a living organism — they are caused, not caught. Common causes are water-logging and starvation.

WEEDS are plants growing where you don't want them to be. Self-sown annual flowers in a Rose bed are weeds, yarrow and speedwell in a wild garden are not.

Prevent problems before they occur

CHOOSE WISELY
Reject soft bulbs, lanky bedding plants, old seeds, unhealthy shrubs and disease-ridden perennials

PLAN CAREFULLY
Make sure that the plant is suited to the site. Avoid sun lovers if shade is a problem — avoid tender types if the garden is exposed and prone to frosts. Rotation of crops is essential for many vegetables

REMOVE DEAD PLANTS, RUBBISH & WEEDS
Rotting plants can be a source of infection — some actually attract pests to the garden. Boxes, old flower pots etc are a breeding ground for slugs and woodlice. Rake away fallen Rose and Apple leaves in winter. Remove Brussels Sprouts and Broccoli stems after harvest. Keep down weeds

PRUNE PROPERLY
You must learn this essential art. It is obviously necessary for ensuring regular fruit and flower production, but it is also important in the war against pests and diseases. Cut out dead wood. Remove overcrowded branches to ensure adequate ventilation. Paint large cuts with Arbrex

USE A PEST BARRIER WHERE POSSIBLE
A number of animals and insects can be kept off plants by using barriers or traps. Use netting to protect seedlings, vegetables and soft fruit. A cylinder of wire-netting around the trunk is the best way to keep squirrels, rabbits, cats and dogs away from the base of trees. Boltac Grease Bands around the trunks of Apple trees will save fruit from the winter moth caterpillar (see page 44) and felt collars around the stems of brassica plants will keep cabbage root fly away. Slug traps can be baited with Slug Pellets (see page 42)

FOLLOW THE RULES OF GOOD HYGIENE UNDER GLASS
The humid atmosphere of a greenhouse is a paradise for pests and diseases. Control is often difficult, so prevention is better than cure. Use compost or sterilised soil. Ensure the house is adequately ventilated; dry air encourages pests and poor growth, saturated air encourages diseases. Try to avoid sudden fluctuations in temperature; water regularly. Water in the morning, although you can water in the early evening if the weather is warm. Remove dead leaves and plants immediately

PLANT OR SOW PROPERLY
Follow the rules for sowing and planting (Chapter 4). These rules will make sure that there will be no air pockets around the roots of new plants and will result in establishment in the minimum possible time. Seed sowing calls for doing the right thing at the right time. Raise flower and vegetable seedlings indoors whenever possible and transplant outdoors when soil and weather are suitable — garden-grown seedlings are more vulnerable to attack

FEED THE PLANTS PROPERLY
Shortage of nutrients can lead to many problems — poor growth, undersized blooms, lowered disease resistance and dis-coloured leaves. But take care — overfeeding can cause scorch and unbalanced feeding with too much nitrogen can result in lots of leaves and very few flowers

PREPARE THE GROUND THOROUGHLY
A strong-growing plant is more likely to withstand pest or disease attack than a weak specimen. Waterlogging due to insufficient soil preparation is the basic cause of failure in heavy soils. Add a humus maker when digging. Read Chapter 2 carefully if you are not a skilled gardener — proper preparation of the soil is essential

Tackle problems promptly when they occur

SPRAY OR DUST PROPERLY

BUY THE RIGHT PRODUCT

- Chemicals for controlling garden troubles are called pesticides. All of these have been thoroughly tested before sale. They are safe to use in the way described on the label — but you must follow the instructions and precautions carefully.
- A bewildering assortment is offered by most garden shops. Before choosing look at the label carefully. This will tell you the active ingredient. Use an organic or mineral pesticide such as a Bio Friendly dust or spray if one is available for the pest or disease to be controlled.

Insecticides

- These products are used to control insects and other small pests. Most organic insecticides work by hitting and killing the pests in question — this calls for spraying during and not before the attack. Use a forceful jet. A few, such as Derris and Quassia, are also leaf-contact insecticides. These work by coating the leaf so that plant-chewing insects such as caterpillars are killed. You don't have to hit the insect but you must cover the surface thoroughly with the spray or dust at the first sign of attack. There are no organic or mineral systemic insecticides — there are only chemical types which can enter the plant's sap stream to kill hidden sap-sucking insects.

Fungicides

- These products are used to control fungal diseases. They are generally preventives and must be used before disease has taken hold. There are no organic systemic fungicides.

Herbicides

- These products are used to control weeds. Always store herbicides away from seeds, plants and other garden products. There are as yet no effective organic herbicides.

USE IT PROPERLY
Before you start

- Read the label carefully. Make sure that the product is recommended for the plant you wish to spray. If it is to be used on a fruit or vegetable check that the harvest interval is acceptable.
- Follow the instructions — do not make the mixture stronger than recommended.

Spraying and Dusting

The weather must be neither sunny nor windy

During the flowering season treat in the evening, when bees will have stopped working

Leaves should be dry

Use a fine forceful spray. It is wise to keep all sprays off your skin. Wash off any splashes

Do not treat open delicate blooms

Spray thoroughly until the leaves are covered with liquid which is just beginning to run off. Dust to provide a fine but complete cover

After you have finished

- Wash out equipment, and wash hands and face.
- Do not keep the spray solution to use next time.
- Store packs in a safe place. Do not keep unlabelled or illegible packs; throw in the dustbin after wrapping in newspaper. Never store in a beer bottle or similar container.

CUT OUT DEAD WOOD

During annual pruning all diseased twigs and branches should be cut off and burnt. If canker is discovered at any time of the year it must be cut out immediately and the wound painted with Arbrex

SPEED RECOVERY WITH A FOLIAR FEED

Plants, like humans, can be invalids. The cause may be a pest or disease. Root action may have been impaired by pest, disease or poor soil conditions. The best way to get things moving again is to use a foliar fertilizer, as the nutrients are instantly absorbed. Fillip is made specifically for this purpose

TAKE EARLY ACTION UNDER GLASS

Trouble can develop quickly under glass, so take immediate action. If spraying is recommended never do it in bright sunlight — after spraying leave the greenhouse and close the door behind you for at least an hour or two. An even better idea for whitefly and other flying insects is to use a Bio Friendly Greenhouse Fly Catcher — see page 44. Place a 2 in. layer of moist peat or compost around stems of Tomatoes and Cucumbers if damaged root action is suspected

PULL UP AND DESTROY IF THE TROUBLE IS INCURABLE

Look closely to find the cause of the trouble. Use the pictures in this book and the Expert books to find out the cause and how to prevent it happening again. Some disease and pest problems (e.g virus, chrysanthemum eelworm, damped off seedlings, root aphid) are incurable. Remove the affected plants and destroy them. Make sure that replanting is permissible before replacing

DON'T TRY TO KILL EVERYTHING

Not all insects are pests — many are positive allies in the war against plant troubles. Obviously these should never be harmed and neither should the major part of the insect population — the ones which are neither friends nor foes. There will be times when plant pests and diseases *will* attack, but even here small infestations of minor pests can be ignored (e.g cuckoo spit) or picked off by hand (e.g caterpillars, rolled leaves, leaf-miner damaged foliage). Spraying or dusting is called for when an important pest is in danger of getting out of hand

Pests

THE BIO FRIENDLY GENERAL INSECTICIDES

	Pest Pistol	Insect Spray	Pest & Disease Duster
Active ingredient(s)	HORTICULTURAL SOAP	DERRIS + QUASSIA	DERRIS + SULPHUR
Uses	Controls whitefly, greenfly, blackfly, red spider mite, scale	Controls greenfly, blackfly, small caterpillars, red spider mite, thrips, flea beetle, raspberry beetle, leaf miner	Controls greenfly, blackfly, small caterpillars, red spider mite, thrips, flea beetle
Notes	Ready-to-use spray. Useful for treating small areas. Safe to ladybirds. Can be used on flowers, shrubs, fruit and vegetables	Dilute 5 ml with 2 pints of water and apply through a sprayer. Useful for treating large areas. Safe to bees but keep away from ponds	Ready-to-use puffer. Apply when infestation begins to build up — repeat as necessary. Safe to bees but keep away from ponds

Surface & Underground Pests

PEST	BACKGROUND	CONTROL
ANTS	Not a serious garden pest, but they can steal seeds and disturb the soil around the roots. Greenfly are carried from one plant to another	Dust along the ant runs and crevices with Bio Friendly Anti-Ant Duster. Contains pyrethrum — use indoors or out
CABBAGE ROOT FLY	Young Cabbages, Sprouts, Radishes, Turnips etc wilt and die — older ones are stunted. Leaves are blue-tinged. Look for small white maggots on the roots	Place a collar around the base of each seedling when planting out if you are really bothered. Lift and destroy affected plants
CARROT FLY	A serious pest of Carrots and Parsnips. Seedlings are killed — mature roots are riddled and liable to rot. Look for reddish leaves and for small creamy maggots in the roots	Try to avoid thinning — the smell of crushed leaves attracts the flies. Next year sow in March or June
CUTWORM	Large grey or brown caterpillars which live just below the surface. Young plants are attacked at night —stems are severed at ground level	July-August is the danger period. Hoe around affected plants — pick up and destroy caterpillars brought to the surface
LEATHERJACKET	Dark grey grubs — 1 in. long and slow moving. Can be a problem on the lawn — look for brown patches and intense bird activity. May also be serious in new, badly-drained plots	Tackle the problem when digging and hoeing. Pick up and destroy the easily-recognisable grubs
ONION FLY	Small white maggots burrow into the bulb bases — young plants are killed, old ones fail to develop. Look for yellow, drooping leaves	Try to avoid thinning — grow sets or transplants. Destroy damaged leaves. Firm the soil around the plants
SLUGS & SNAILS	These are serious garden pests, especially when the weather is wet and cool. They hide under stones and debris during the day and come out at night, devouring seedlings and the roots, stems, leaves and even flowers of a wide range of plants. Slime trails are a tell-tale clue	Remove rubbish and hand-pick at night, but you will need a slug killer if attacks are bad. Mini Slug Pellets (metaldehyde) are popular, but you must use them properly. *Never* put down heaps — spread very thinly around the plants and not all over the soil. Store the pack safely. Read 'Pets' (page 59)
WIREWORM	A pest in newly-broken grassland — ½ in. long shiny, yellow grubs attack the roots of many plants — Potatoes, Chrysanthemums and root crops can suffer badly	Avoid growing Potatoes and root vegetables for about 3 years in infested land. Remove and destroy grubs when digging

Carrot fly

Cutworm

Onion fly

Slugs & Snails

Above-ground Pests

PEST	BACKGROUND	CONTROL
APPLE SAWFLY	A ribbon-like scar appears on the skin. A creamy grub is inside — sticky 'frass' surrounds the surface hole. Fruit usually drops in July	Pick up and destroy fallen fruit. Use Insect Spray a few days after petal fall
BLACKFLY	A serious pest of Broad Beans in spring and French Beans in July. Large colonies stunt growth, damage flowers and distort pods	Pinch out tops of Broad Beans once 5 flower trusses have formed. Use Pest Pistol or Insect Spray
CATERPILLARS	Many types attack plants — usual sign is the presence of large irregular holes in the leaves. Cabbage white butterfly can be serious	If practical pick off by hand. Where damage is widespread use Insect Spray or Pest & Disease Duster
CODLING MOTH	Pale pink grubs can be found inside fruits of Apples, Pears and Plums in July and August. Sawdust-like 'frass' surrounds eaten-out area	Live with it. The only practical alternative is to use a chemical spray programme
CUCKOO SPIT	Frothy white musses occur on the stems of many plants. Within is the cause — pinkish ⅛ in. long frog-hoppers which suck the sap	Wash off with a forceful jet of water if you wish, but not really worth bothering about
EARWIG	A pest without many friends, although it is harmless. It can attack vegetables and fruit — Chrysanthemums and Dahlias are the major targets. Leaves and petals are torn	Shake plants — destroy earwigs which fall. Trap in upturned flower pots filled with straw
EELWORM	Eelworms are microscopic worms which affect leaves, stems or roots. Chrysanthemum eelworm causes brown areas between veins — potato eelworm stunts growth	See appropriate Expert book for identification. No cure — do not replant for 3–6 years
FLEA BEETLE	Tiny yellow and black beetles which jump when disturbed. Small round holes appear in young leaves of the Cabbage family. Not serious on older plants	Use Insect Spray or Pest & Disease Duster if the attack is serious. Spray affected plants with Fillip
GREENFLY	An all-too-familiar pest — green, brown, yellow or pink. Rapid build-up in warm, settled weather. Young growth is weakened — viruses are transmitted	Water plants in dry weather. Spray greenfly clusters with Pest Pistol or Insect Spray
LEAFHOPPER	Small green insect produces pale mottled patches on leaves of ornamentals, e.g Pelargonium. Direct damage is slight but viruses are transmitted	The insects are killed by derris but spraying or dusting is not worth-while
LEAF MINER	Winding tunnels, blisters or blotches occur on the leaves of many plants, including Chrysanthemums and Carnations	Pick off and destroy mined leaves. Celery fly (brown blisters) can be serious — never plant seedlings with brown leaves
MEALY BUG	An indoor pest, infesting house plants and greenhouse ornamentals. Clusters of white, cottony fluff occur on stems and the underside of leaves	Deal with the trouble promptly. Wipe off with a damp cloth or a moistened cotton bud
PEA & BEAN WEEVIL	No problem with older plants, but young Peas and Beans can be killed or severely retarded by the small beetles which bite notches in the leaves	Hoe around plants in April and May. Use Insect Spray if the attack is severe

Blackfly

Codling moth

Chrysanthemum eelworm

Flea beetle

Leaf miner

Pea & bean weevil

Above-ground Pests contd.

PEST	BACKGROUND	CONTROL
PEA MOTH	The cause of maggoty Peas. Eggs are laid on the leaves in summer — the greenish grubs bore through the pods and into the seeds	Early- and late-sown crops usually escape damage. Otherwise use Insect Spray 7–10 days after flowering starts
RASPBERRY BEETLE	The cause of maggoty Raspberries, Loganberries and Blackberries. The ¼ in. grubs can soon ruin the crop. A serious pest	If attacks occurred last year, use Insect Spray when the first fruits start to turn pink
RED SPIDER MITE	A general pest which can be serious on fruit, greenhouse and house plants. Leaves turn an unhealthy bronze — fine silky webbing is a tell-tale sign	Encouraged by hot and dry conditions. Damp down under glass. Use Insect Spray, Pest & Disease Duster or Pest Pistol
ROOT APHID	Greyish 'greenfly' and white powdery patches occur on the roots. Many plants can be affected but Lettuce is the favourite host. Growth is stunted	There is no cure. Lift and destroy affected plants. Grow aphid-resistant Lettuce variety (e.g Avoncrisp)
ROSE SLUGWORM	Areas of the leaf are skeletonised as only the soft tissues and not the veins are eaten. Affected areas turn brown. Greenish grubs on surface	Pick off affected leaves. If serious use Insect Spray
SCALE	Non-moving insects which attack a wide range of plants. The small discs are found on stems and the underside of leaves — a scaly crust may be present	Wipe off with a damp cloth or a moistened cotton bud. Pest Pistol is the spray to use
THRIPS	Silvery flecking and streaking occur on flowers, leaves and pods — Pea pods are distorted. Minute black or yellow flies are just visible	Not usually treated, but any Bio Friendly spray or dust (see page 42) will control them
WASPS	A pest in the home, of course, but also a nuisance in the garden as ripening tree and soft fruits are damaged. Only blemished fruit is attacked	Live with the problem. If close to the house it may be necessary to destroy the nest
WHITEFLY	Cabbage whitefly has become a serious pest of brassicas in the past few years. Plants are weakened and black moulds develop. Attacks can occur at any time of the year	Not easy to control. The best plan is to spray with Pest Pistol at weekly intervals as long as attacks persist
WINTER MOTH	Green 'looper' caterpillars devour the young leaves of fruit trees. Petals, flower stalks and fruitlets may also be attacked. Leaves are often spun together	Encircle each trunk with a Boltac Grease Band in autumn and keep in place until April
WOOLLY APHID	A pest of ornamental and fruit trees and shrubs — the white waxy wool on the stems is produced by the aphids within. Corky galls form on affected shoots	Rub or scrape off — brush large areas with an old tooth-brush and methylated spirits

Pea moth

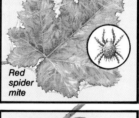

Raspberry beetle

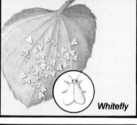

Red spider mite

Whitefly

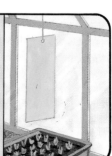

Woolly aphid

Check that Pest!
Don't assume every brown leaf and creepy crawly means a pest attack — check in the appropriate Expert

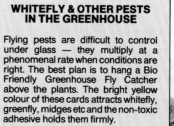

WHITEFLY & OTHER PESTS IN THE GREENHOUSE

Flying pests are difficult to control under glass — they multiply at a phenomenal rate when conditions are right. The best plan is to hang a Bio Friendly Greenhouse Fly Catcher above the plants. The bright yellow colour of these cards attracts whitefly, greenfly, midges etc and the non-toxic adhesive holds them firmly.

Animal Pests

A number of animals can damage your garden, but the approach to them must be different to the way we tackle insect pests. The object here must be to protect the plants and/or discourage the invaders without causing them actual harm. There are exceptions — rats must be killed and the mole too, if all else fails.

PEST	BACKGROUND	CONTROL
BIRDS	Birds can be a nuisance nearly all the year round. The flower garden is least affected — only Polyanthus, Primula Wanda and Crocus are stripped of buds and flowers. Vegetables can suffer badly, especially Peas and the Cabbage family. Seeds and seedlings are eaten, sparrows tear flowers and pods, and pigeons strip away the soft portion of leaves and foul Broccoli etc with their droppings. Bullfinches and sparrows devour buds of Cherries, Plums, Gooseberries etc — the fruit is also attacked	Small areas can be protected with soft plastic netting — make sure all the plants are covered and the base of the net is properly secured. For a large number of plants a fruit cage is undoubtedly the best answer. Spray-on repellants are of limited value and are removed by rain — mechanical scarers soon lose their ability to frighten away birds
CATS	Cats are a pest of the flower and vegetable garden. Seed beds and young transplants are disturbed by their scratching. The resulting root damage can lead to the death of the seedlings	Protection is not easy if cats have chosen your flower bed as a toilet. Sprinkle Pepper Dust liberally around the disturbed ground
DEER	Deer can be a serious pest in rural areas close to woodland. Young trees are grazed — the bark may be stripped in winter. Rose buds are a favourite meal	Tall fencing is the real answer but may not be practical. Ring the trunks of trees with fine-mesh wire netting
DOGS	Dogs, like cats, will scratch in soft ground. Remove dog droppings at once — they are a health risk. The most serious effect, however, is the brown patches caused on lawns by bitch urine	Hedges and prickly shrubs will deter stray dogs. Pepper Dust is a deterrent. Copiously water affected areas on the lawn
FOXES	A new but not serious pest in urban areas — plants are not attacked but dustbins are disturbed. Holes are occasionally scratched in lawns	Do not leave plastic bags containing waste food standing out overnight. Fit secure lids to dustbins
MICE, RATS & VOLES	Mice, rats and voles attack stored fruits and vegetables — in the garden whole rows of larger seeds such as Peas may be removed	Rats *must* be destroyed. If you see one then get in touch with the Council. Use Racumin for mice and voles — follow the instructions precisely
MOLES	An invasion by moles can cause havoc. Severe root damage occurs and the hills thrown up by their tunnelling are unsightly and small plants may be uprooted. The lawn is most at risk — the surface is disfigured and rendered uneven	Begin with simple remedies. Moles dislike soil disturbance — try a mechanical scarer. Next, try an anti-mole smoke. If all else fails you may have to call in a professional exterminator. Don't put down poison or traps yourself
RABBITS	Rabbits are very fond of young greens, but in winter they will gnaw the bark at the base of trees. A serious problem in rural areas — they can easily burrow underneath ordinary fencing	Individual tree guards (see deer above) can be used, but an anti-rabbit fence is the only complete answer. The wire netting is 3 ft above ground, and 6 in. below. The bottom of the fence extends horizontally for about 6 in.
SQUIRRELS	Nice to watch, but they can be a nuisance. Bulbs, soft fruit, nuts etc are removed and bark is stripped in winter	There is little you can do. Fruit netting helps and wire-netting tree guards will protect individual trees — bend the top of the cylinder away from the trunk

Birds

Cats

Moles

Rabbits

Diseases

Disease control is difficult if you restrict yourself to 'natural' products. Only two basic types are available — copper and sulphur. Neither are organic, but both are simple products which have been used for generations. They are protectants and not cures and do not have the power of modern systemic chemicals.

Bio Friendly Pest & Disease Duster

Active ingredient	COPPER	SULPHUR
Uses	Controls downy mildews, blights, some rusts	Controls powdery mildews, storage rots
Notes	Cheshunt Compound is a copper fungicide used to control damping off of seedlings	Ready-to-use puffer. Apply to Roses, ornamentals and fruit before disease takes hold. Safe to bees but keep away from fish

DISEASE	BACKGROUND	CONTROL
APPLE SCAB	A serious disease of Apples and Pears. Appears first as dark green or brown spots on leaves and blistered shoots. Fruits are cracked and disfigured with corky patches	Rake up and remove fallen leaves. Prune scabby twigs. Dusting at green bud and petal fall with Pest & Disease Duster will help
BACTERIAL CANKER	A serious disease of Cherries, Plums and other stone fruit. Gum oozes from the bark — affected branches produce few leaves and soon die	Cut out diseased branches — paint cuts with Arbrex. Spray with copper in autumn
BLACK SPOT	A major Rose problem — black spots with yellow fringes on the leaves. These spots may spread rapidly and premature leaf fall often takes place	Rake and dispose of all fallen leaves in winter — apply a mulch in spring. Sulphur will help — use as the leaves are opening and again in summer
BROWN ROT	Apples and most tree fruit are susceptible. Fruit turns brown and concentric rings of yellowish mould appear on the surface	Destroy all affected fruit promptly. Store only sound fruit and inspect at regular intervals
BULB, CORM & TUBER ROTS	Browning and decay of underground storage organs — may occur in store or in the ground. Fungal growth is sometimes seen on the surface	Dry thoroughly and use Pest & Disease Duster before storing. Discard any soft or rotten bulbs
CANKER	A serious disease of Apples and Pears which can be fatal. Bark shrinks and cracks in concentric rings. Red growths in winter	Cut off damaged twigs. Cut out canker from stems and branches. Paint cuts with Arbrex
CLUB ROOT	Swollen and distorted roots are the tell-tale sign of this disease of Stocks, Wallflowers and all the Cabbage family. Leaves wilt in sunny weather — growth is very slow	Make sure land is adequately limed and well-drained — remove plants promptly after harvest. Lift and destroy diseased plants — do not replant for several years
DAMPING OFF	The most serious seedling complaint. The base of an affected plant becomes withered and blackened — the stem topples over	Use sterilised compost, sow thinly and never overwater. Remove affected seedlings and water remainder with Cheshunt Compound
DIE-BACK	A common problem with woody plants such as Roses, fruit trees, ornamental shrubs etc. The stem tip dies and spreads slowly downwards	Cut out all dead wood. Paint all cuts with Arbrex and try to improve drainage
DOWNY MILDEWS	Less likely to be troublesome than powdery mildew in the ornamental garden, but it can be serious on the vegetable plot. Upper leaf surface turns yellow — greyish mould occurs below	Make sure the soil is well-drained — practice crop rotation of vegetables. Pick off diseased leaves
GREY MOULD (Botrytis)	Grey and fluffy mould appears on stems, leaves, flowers and soft fruit. Worst outdoors in a wet season and in unventilated damp conditions under glass	Avoid the basic causes — poor drainage, overwatering and inadequate ventilation. Remove affected leaves and fruit

Apple scab

Tuber rot

Club root

Damping off

Grey mould

DISEASE	BACKGROUND	CONTROL
LEAF SPOT	Blotches, spots or rings appear on leaves — especially Celery and Blackcurrant. Leaves may fall early. See Expert books for identification	Feed with a fertilizer containing potash. Pick off diseased leaves and avoid overcrowding
PEACH LEAF CURL	Large reddish blisters develop on the foliage of Peaches, Cherries, Apricots etc. Unsightly, and the tree is weakened. Early leaf fall occurs	There is not much you can do, so expect attacks every year. Pick off and destroy affected leaves promptly
POTATO BLIGHT	Spreading brown patches appear on the leaves and infected tubers rot in store. Attacks occur in warm, wet weather. Tomatoes can be affected	Spray with copper every 2 weeks if attack starts early. Remove infected stems a fortnight before lifting. Inspect the stored crop
POTATO SCAB	Ragged scurf patches occur on the tuber surface. The disease is only skin-deep — eating quality unaffected. Worst on light land and in dry weather	Use compost but not lime before planting. Grow a resistant variety
POWDERY MILDEW	A general menace all round the garden. White powdery deposit occurs on the leaves, stems, buds and fruit. Worst in hot, dry weather. Serious on Roses	Mulch in spring and water during dry periods in summer. Dust regularly with Pest & Disease Duster once first spots appear on Roses
ROOT & FOOT ROTS	Many plants, especially vegetables, can succumb. Leaves wilt and turn yellow — roots and some-times the stem bases blacken and rot. Often fatal	Avoid cold and overwet conditions. Use a sterile compost. Rotate vegetable crops. Lift and destroy infected plants
RUST	Raised pustules (orange, brown or black) appear on the leaves. Numerous plants may be attacked, but Rose rust is the one to fear — attacks may be fatal	Use a fertilizer containing potash. Remove affected leaves. Sulphur may help, but if Roses are attacked you must use the modern systemic Systhane
SOOTY MOULD	A black fungus which spots or covers the upper surface of the foliage. Grows on the honeydew deposited by sap-sucking pests	Wash off if unsightly. Control by spraying or dusting to get rid of greenfly etc
STEM ROT	A brown patch develops at or near the stem base — roots are not affected. This disease can be serious on Tomatoes	Disinfect the greenhouse between Tomato crops. Cut out diseased area if attack is slight. Remove and destroy plant if badly affected
STORAGE ROTS	Soft grey or brown sunken areas appear on Apples and Pears in store. Mould often develops on the affected patches	Discard unsound fruit at storage time. Remove and destroy diseased fruit promptly
TULIP FIRE	Scorched areas occur on the leaves — flowers are spotted. Young shoots are covered with a grey, velvety mould and the bulbs rot	Diseased shoots should be cut off just below ground level. There is no cure
VIRUS	All sorts of distortions, discolorations and growth problems are produced, depending on the plant. See Expert books for identification	No cure. Destroy infected plants if you are sure of identification. Keep sap-sucking insects under control
WHITE ROT	The leaves of Onions and Leeks turn yellow and wilt. Fluffy white mould appears on the base of the bulbs. Growth is stunted. Worst in hot, dry weather	Rotate crops. Destroy diseased plants — do not replant with Onions or Leeks for at least 8 years
WILT	Several wilt fungi can attack vegetable and ornamental plants. Leaves wilt even in moist soil and tissue inside stems is often stained brown	No cure — do not grow susceptible plants in the same soil. See Expert books for identification

Peach leaf curl

Powdery mildew

Rust

Tulip fire

White rot

Wilt

Disorders

Not all troubles are caused by pests and diseases — split Tomatoes, heartless Cabbages and bolted Beetroots do not appear in the pest charts but they are still the effects of important disorders. These disorders are due to faults in cultivation or an adverse environment. It is important to try to find the cause because many of them can be prevented once you know what went wrong. Important disorders and their causes are listed below, but there are others. Bitterness in greenhouse Cucumbers is generally due to failure to remove male flowers, blindness of Tulips and Daffodils is usually due to planting undersized bulbs, and the forking of Carrots is due to poorly prepared ground or the application of a raw humus maker.

DISORDER	BACKGROUND
BOLTING	A number of vegetables have the annoying habit of occasionally bolting or running to seed. The cause is a set-back to steady growth, so try to avoid checks. Prepare the soil properly, plant out firmly and at the right time and make sure the plants are watered in dry weather. Lettuce, Onion, Celery and Beetroot are prone to bolting — grow a bolt-resistant variety if you can
DROUGHT	See page 28
DRY AIR DAMAGE	In the home or greenhouse the effect is a browning of leaf tips. Both outdoors and indoors the most obvious result is a poor set of vegetables which form fruit or pods — Tomatoes, Beans etc. Misting flowers at pollination time helps Tomatoes but not Beans
FROST DAMAGE	With non-hardy plants frost threatens life itself — transplant or sow when the danger of frost is past. A hard frost can damage the tender new growth of hardy plants such as Potatoes, Asparagus, Apple etc. Affected leaves may be bleached, blistered, cracked or scorched along the margins. The worst effects of frost are seen in the fruit garden — blossom turns brown and drops off. A late severe frost can be devastating to Pears, Plums etc
INCORRECT PLANTING	Incorrect planting can lead to slow development or even death of transplants — do follow the rules on pages 32–33. Inadequate soil consolidation and loose planting lead to several distinct disorders in the vegetable garden — blown Brussels Sprouts, heartless Cabbages, button-headed Cauliflowers etc
IRREGULAR WATERING DAMAGE	The outer skin of many vegetables hardens under drought conditions, and when heavy rain or watering takes place the sudden increase in growth stretches and then splits the skin. This results in the splitting of Tomatoes, Potatoes, Carrots etc. Avoid by watering before the soil dries out. A common disorder due to the irregular watering of growing bags is blossom end rot — a sunken, dark-coloured patch appears at the bottom of Tomatoes
MAJOR NUTRIENT SHORTAGE	See page 36
SUN & HEAT DAMAGE	Bright sunshine can damage plants grown under glass. Leaves and fruit may be scorched — the pale papery patches are referred to as sun scald. The answer is to apply shading material such as Coolglass in summer. Tomatoes suffer from too much sun and heat. Disorders include greenback (area around the stalk remains hard and green) and blotchy ripening (parts of the fruit remain yellow or orange)
TRACE ELEMENT SHORTAGE	Leaf discoloration is a common symptom. Iron and manganese deficiency lead to yellowing between the veins — the effect is most marked in non-acid soils. Several vegetable disorders are due to trace element shortage. Examples include browning of Cauliflower curd and brown heart of Turnip (boron deficiency) and marsh spot of Peas (manganese deficiency)
WATERLOGGING	The plant is affected in 2 ways. Root development is crippled by the shortage of air in the soil. The root system becomes shallow, and also ineffective as the root hairs die. Leaves turn pale and growth is stunted. The second serious effect is the stimulation of root-rotting diseases. Read Chapter 2 carefully
WEEDKILLER DRIFT	Traces of hormone lawn weedkiller can cause severe distortion of Tomatoes and members of the Cabbage family. Tomato leaves become fern-like and twisted. Fruit is plum-shaped and hollow. Avoid trouble by applying lawn weedkiller on a still day. Never use lawn weedkiller equipment for any other purpose
WIND DAMAGE	Wind is often ignored as a danger to plant growth, yet a cold east wind in spring can kill in the same way as frost. More frequently the effect is the browning of leaf margins. Strong winds can inhibit the activity of pollinating insects — poor fruit set is the result in the fruit garden. Another damaging effect is wind rock, which can lead to rotting of the roots

Frost damage

Irregular watering damage

Manganese shortage

Sun & heat damage

Weeds

Weeds have no place in a well-ordered garden — even a Bio Friendly one. Have a wildflower area by all means, but that is not the same thing as having rampant weeds swamping your garden plants and competing for water, nutrients and light. Worst of all they give the garden a neglected look. So the menace of weeds must be tackled, and tackled quickly before they take hold. Many efficient weedkillers are available, but these are nearly all modern chemicals. The Bio Friendly gardener uses them in a limited way and only when really necessary — the main approach is to use a combination of some of the non-chemical methods shown below.

ANNUAL WEEDS complete at least one life cycle during the season. They spread by seeding, and all fertile soils contain a large reservoir of annual weed seeds. The golden rule is that emerged annuals must be killed *before* seeding by hand pulling, hoeing or burning off with a contact weedkiller. **A**

PERENNIAL WEEDS survive by means of underground stems or roots which act as storage organs over winter. The golden rule is that their leaves must be regularly removed to starve out the underground storage organs or else a translocated weedkiller must be used. **P**

HAND PULLING
The oldest method of control and still a useful technique in certain situations. It includes the removal of well-grown but easily uprooted annual weeds in beds and borders, the digging out of isolated deep-rooted weeds in the lawn and the eradication of weeds growing amongst the alpines in the rockery. A technique to consider where there are a few large weeds, but not when the problem is widespread and serious.

HOEING
The hoe is the traditional enemy of the emerged weed, and despite all the advances of science it still remains the most important weedkilling technique around growing plants. It is much quicker than hand pulling, and will destroy large numbers of annual weeds if the soil surface is dry, the hoe blade is sharp and the depth of cut kept shallow. Not really effective against perennials — hoe at regular intervals to starve out roots.

MULCHING
Read the mulching section on page 9. Organic mulches will help to suppress annual weeds, but the use of a black polythene mulch for weed control is even more spectacular. A weed-infested patch can be covered, the surface hidden with bark chippings, gravel or peat, and no weeds will peep through for years.

FLAME GUNNING
An oversized blow torch for burning off the top growth of weeds and destroying surface seeds — once fairly popular but not often used these days. This is not a technique for the Bio Friendly garden — there is a risk in careless hands. In addition the intense heat is lethal to the many insects which live just below the surface, and organic matter in this zone is destroyed.

DIGGING
Weed control begins at the digging stage. The roots of perennial weeds should be removed and burnt. The surface layer of annual weeds should be buried by inverting the spadeful of soil. This is not the end of the problem — weed seeds buried many years previously can be brought to the surface by the digging operation.

HERBICIDES
During the past 30 years many weedkillers have appeared, both contact ones which burn off the above-ground parts and trans-located types which get down to the roots. Bio Friendly gardeners generally restrict their use to overall treatment of the grass in spring with a lawn sand such as Velvas, and then spot treatment of perennial weeds around the garden with a product like the Bio Weed Pencil.

GROUND COVER
Creeping evergreens with leafy stems provide an excellent way of suppressing weed growth on bare ground. Choose easy-to-grow varieties with thornless stems, although some of the new ground-cover Roses such as Grouse are becoming popular, despite their thorny and deciduous nature. Well known ground cover plants include Euonymus, Vinca, Erica, Cotoneaster and Ajuga. Make sure the area is free from weeds before planting.

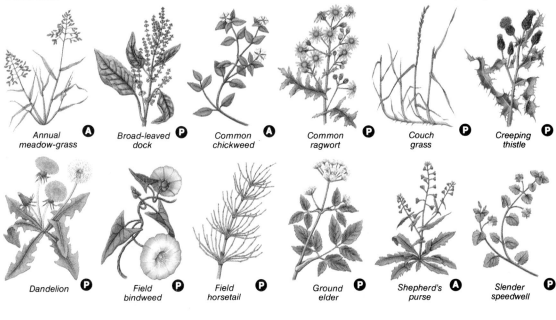

Annual meadow-grass **A**   *Broad-leaved dock* **P**   *Common chickweed* **A**   *Common ragwort* **P**   *Couch grass* **P**   *Creeping thistle* **P**

Dandelion **P**   *Field bindweed* **P**   *Field horsetail* **P**   *Ground elder* **P**   *Shepherd's purse* **A**   *Slender speedwell* **P**

CHAPTER 6
People Friendly —
AVOIDING THE DANGER SPOTS

Few pastimes can match the health-giving properties of gardening and the feeling of satisfaction it gives when the day is over. For millions it is a time to escape from mental stress and to indulge in physical exercise which the working day may deny.

Against this background it is hard to talk about the dangers of gardening, but facts must be faced. Each year about 400,000 people have an accident, and of these approximately 250,000 need hospital treatment. A shocking figure, but the consoling thought is that in nearly every case the cause is either ignorance or carelessness. In about three quarters of the incidents involving adult gardeners the cause is known at once and the patient knows what he or she has done wrong. Unlike flying, driving, playing rugby etc your safety and that of your family is in your own hands, and by following a number of rules you can avoid becoming an accident statistic.

First of all, get rid of hazards. Level paths which are uneven, fix loose stones, hang up tools, remove dangerous branches etc. Next, wear suitable clothing. Footwear must always be right for the job — gloves and goggles may be required. Then learn how to use equipment before you start — read the instructions carefully. Finally, think what you are doing. As an excellent leaflet by the Royal Society for the Prevention of Accidents said some years ago "when attention is concentrated on the job, sensible precautions are often forgotten".

Accidents cannot be prevented by going green — the table below shows it is not a green v. non-green issue. It all began right at the beginning, when Eve ate a poisonous fruit in the garden and Cain was felled by the improper use of a spade.

The Causes of Accidents

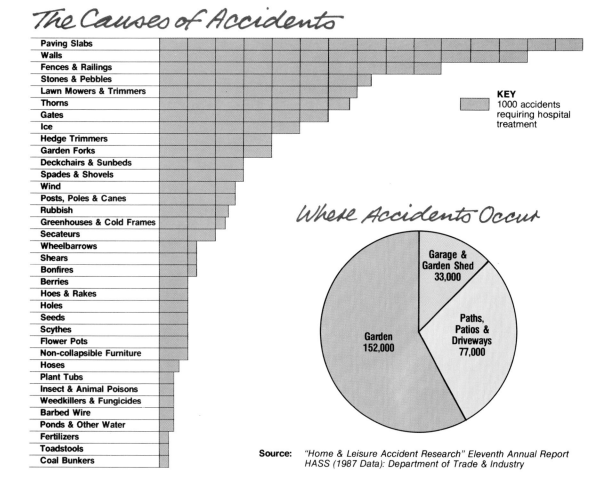

KEY
☐ 1000 accidents requiring hospital treatment

Paving Slabs
Walls
Fences & Railings
Stones & Pebbles
Lawn Mowers & Trimmers
Thorns
Gates
Ice
Hedge Trimmers
Garden Forks
Deckchairs & Sunbeds
Spades & Shovels
Wind
Posts, Poles & Canes
Rubbish
Greenhouses & Cold Frames
Secateurs
Wheelbarrows
Shears
Bonfires
Berries
Hoes & Rakes
Holes
Seeds
Scythes
Flower Pots
Non-collapsible Furniture
Hoses
Plant Tubs
Insect & Animal Poisons
Weedkillers & Fungicides
Barbed Wire
Ponds & Other Water
Fertilizers
Toadstools
Coal Bunkers

Where Accidents Occur

Garage & Garden Shed 33,000

Paths, Patios & Driveways 77,000

Garden 152,000

Source: "Home & Leisure Accident Research" Eleventh Annual Report HASS (1987 Data): Department of Trade & Industry

Being People Friendly to Children

Getting children out from under your feet and into the garden is often a great relief for you and them. A chance to play in the open air, but sombre accident statistics tell us that about 100,000 children are treated in hospital each year as a result of mishaps in the garden. Some are fatal, yet nearly all are avoidable if you follow a few commonsense rules.

The danger time is the toddler stage. Between the ages of 2 and 5 children are active with little sense of danger. It is therefore necessary to keep dangerous objects out of their reach and out of their path. You should supervise them at play if danger areas are present.

PLAY AREA

Play should be a danger-free activity, but 5,000 toddlers go to hospital each year as a result of an accident on outdoor play equipment such as a swing or slide.

Siting of a play area is important — place it in sight of the kitchen window if possible. The surface is even more important — use a base of sand, rubber pads, a 4 in. layer of shredded bark or grass. Never put a swing, climbing frame or slide on stone or concrete.

Buy equipment made to a British Standard specification. Secure firmly and maintain regularly. Swings are the major cause of accidents — make sure children don't stand too close when waiting for their turn.

WATER

A toddler can drown in 3 inches of water — never allow a child under 3 to go near an unguarded pond or into a paddling pool without supervision. This doesn't only apply to your own children — half of the accidents involving water happen to children in other people's gardens.

Some basic rules. Protect a pond with a fence or wire mesh cover if children play nearby — consider turning it into a sand pit if protection is impractical. Empty paddling pools when not in use and cover water butts.

KEEP OUT OF HARM'S WAY

Tools & machinery should be kept away from children, especially when in use. Mowing, pruning, hedge trimming and spraying are strictly grown-up jobs where little helping hands should be discouraged. Hang up cultivating tools in the garden shed or garage and keep cutting tools out of reach.

Paths are for walking — the lawn is for running. Cycling, roller-skating and skate-boarding are too dangerous in a small garden and should be discouraged. Keep paths free from moss, algae and lichens, and make sure that toys and equipment are moved before someone trips over them.

Seeds & plants may be poisonous. Teach young children not to eat *any* berries, leaves etc — later on you can show them the dangerous ones (see page 57). Remember not to set a bad example by picking and eating fruit and vegetables when in the garden with small children.

Chemicals, DIY products & flammable liquids should be kept well out of the way — see page 56.

GATES & FENCES

You must make sure that small children can't wander into the road. In most gardens this calls for secure fencing and a gate which can be locked beyond the reach or ability of little fingers. Fencing is not possible in an open-plan garden — constant supervision is the only answer here. Do not go away and trust to the good sense of a toddler or small child.

GLASS

Glass and children definitely don't mix — both can harm each other. Balls can break glass — glass can cause horrific injuries to a colliding child. Try to keep the greenhouse and cold frame as far away as possible from the area where children play, and don't leave objects on which children (and you) can trip close to patio windows, greenhouses etc.

You should really think about extra precautions if you have active children or grandchildren who play in the garden. This calls for using a shatterproof glass substitute for both greenhouse and cold frame. If this is not feasible then you should certainly glaze or cover the lower part of a greenhouse with safety glass, PVC, wood or brick.

CAT & DOG DROPPINGS

Parasites occur in about a quarter of cat and dog droppings. These rarely affect human beings, but if they do the effect can be extremely serious. As a result children are admitted to hospital every year, and you should therefore dispose of droppings promptly without handling them. It is especially important to cover a sand pit when not in use — pets regard an uncovered one as a most desirable toilet.

Being People Friendly to You

Falls account for one in every two accidents in the area around the house, which is surprisingly high. There are falls due to tools or toys being left lying about, falls due to improper use of ladders and falls on slimy or icy paths.

Most falls result in a bump or sprain and do not require hospital treatment, but many are serious and some are fatal. So take care, especially if you are over 60 years old. A fall can affect any area of the body, but some mishaps are specific to a particular part and are described on these two pages.

CLOTHING

Correct clothing is important. It should keep you warm and protected in winter — cool and protected in summer. The key word is 'protected'. Avoid loose bits like ties and scarves when working with fast-moving machinery.

Head protection is not usually necessary, but you will need an industrial hard hat if you are planning to lop off tree branches which are more than head-high. It is also a good idea to wear a brimmed hat to keep branches off your face when working amongst trees — e.g pruning, spraying and harvesting.

Ear protectors are recommended if you are using a noisy power tool for a prolonged period. Remember the neighbours do not have ear protectors — try to agree with them the best time to do a really noisy job. **Goggles** are sometimes necessary — see the Eyes section.

Gloves are necessary to protect your hands when undertaking many garden tasks, and you may need more than one type. Leather gloves protect against prickles, sharp objects and caustic materials such as lime. The problem is that they are heavy, rather inflexible and uncomfortable in hot weather. Cotton gloves are much more comfortable but are no protection against Rose thorns. You will need gauntlets if you propose to use a chainsaw, and rubber gloves if you plan to handle corrosive or toxic liquids. Most people compromise by using all-purpose gloves — fabric ones with leather palms or fabric gloves impregnated with green plastic.

Stout **footwear** is essential when digging, forking, mowing and carrying heavy loads. Wellington boots are a popular choice — choosing ones with reinforced toes and protective shin guards has prevented many accidents. When working in the garden in winter your shoes or boots must be warm and completely waterproof.

HANDS

Bruises are commonplace and generally look after themselves. Cuts definitely do not — they require immediate attention. The simple drill is to wash out any dirt immediately with soap and warm water after which the wound should be covered with a porous elastic dressing or absorbent gauze and a bandage. Do not use an airtight plaster. Remove splinters or embedded thorns with a needle which has been sterilized by immersion in boiling water.

Prevention, of course, is always better than cure. Wear gloves when handling soil as buried bits of glass or broken pots can result in a nasty gash. Make sure that the branches of thorny bushes do not overhang pathways. Handle glass with great care. If you are a regular gardener and just cannot seem to avoid picking up cuts and scratches, a routine anti-tetanus injection really is a good idea. The bacterium which causes the disease lives in the soil and its effects are serious — several people die each year from tetanus.

Most cuts require neither a doctor nor hospital treatment, but if blood loss is excessive you should seek medical help immediately. This also applies if a home-treated cut starts to hurt after a day or two or the area around becomes swollen or discoloured.

EYES

Serious eye injuries are perhaps the most distressing mishaps of all. Do take simple precautions. Place a small cream or yoghurt pot on top of each cane in areas where you will be working amongst the plants — people really do bend down and drive bamboo canes into their eyes. Remove stones from the grass before using a power mower and be careful of twigs and branches when pruning trees.

More than one in 10 people who garden or carry out DIY jobs at home injure their eyes at some time. To avoid problems you should wear goggles when doing any job which has a history of accidents — drilling holes in masonry, cutting tiles or concrete slabs, using an axe, hedge clipping, using a chainsaw, lopping trees etc.

FEET

Pushing a garden fork through one's foot is an all-too-common occurrence — each year 4000 accidents requiring hospital treatment are caused by the improper use of a fork. There are two rules to follow. You must protect your feet properly — sandals, track shoes etc are definitely out when using a digging tool or a lawn mower. Stout boots or shoes are essential — see Clothing section above. You must also keep your mind on what you are doing when digging, forking or cutting the lawn — carelessness is nearly always involved in foot injury.

BACK

Falls are the major cause of gardening accidents requiring hospital treatment, but it is back strain which is by far the most common reason for discomfort and days off work. Most gardening problems arise from carelessness, but back strain is different. The problem here has three causes. Lack of knowledge concerning the right way to prepare for bending and lifting, incorrect posture when carrying out the tasks, or doing the wrong thing when the job is over. Do read the instructions below even if you are an experienced gardener — few people know all the rules.

Before you begin

Spring is the worst time, as any physiotherapist will tell you. Muscles which may have been inactive for months are suddenly called into play, and the weather is usually cold. It is therefore a good idea to carry out a simple exercise programme before going out to dig or plant — consider it essential and not just a good idea if you are over forty, have a sedentary job and it is early in the year. This calls for bending over and then stretching back several times whilst standing with your legs apart. Then bend from side to side and tense your buttocks for a few seconds. Repeat several times and you are ready to go.

When you are working

Make sure your clothing is right. You should be warm and comfortable with no part of your back exposed to cold winds. Try to remain as upright as possible with the back arched. This calls for digging and cultivating tools with handles which are longer than you might be used to, and cutting the grass with the mower handles held close to the body. With a hover mower move the machine backwards and forwards — never side to side. Kneeling instead of stooping is the golden rule, and never jerk suddenly to pull up a weed or lift up a load. Try to vary the heavy jobs — don't do any strenuous task for more than half an hour at one time.

After you have finished

Clean the tools, put them away safely and *don't* flop in a chair. Muscles must be stretched after work if backache the next morning is to be avoided. Sit upright in a straight chair for a little while if the jobs have not been particularly strenuous — put a rolled-up towel between the chair and the small of your back. You should do instead some stretching exercises if you've had a physically exhausting day. Lie on your back. Lift your right leg in the air and lower it to the floor on your left-hand side. Put your legs together and now do the exercise with your left leg. Repeat the procedure 10 times.

Lifting

Back straight

Make sure the load is not too heavy. Divide up if possible

Knees bent

Feet 1–1½ ft apart on either side of the load

Shoulders back

Keep the load close to your body

Elbows close to the thighs

Use leg muscles to lift the load

Make sure you can see where you are going

Hoeing & Raking

Handle long enough to avoid stooping

Back straight and slightly arched

Feet spaced apart

Weeding & Planting

Hoe rather than hand pull weeds if you are over 50 and/or suffer from back trouble

Keep close to the plant — don't stretch too far forward or sideways

Don't stoop or bend — kneel on a soft mat. Sit on a low stool instead of kneeling if your knees are arthritic

Digging & Forking

Read the Digging section — page 5

Handle long enough to avoid stooping

Back straight and slightly arched

Let your legs do the work rather than your back

Being People Friendly with
Tools & Furniture

A wide range of tools and equipment is listed in the accident chart on page 50. Cutting, digging and cultivating tools have always posed a risk to the young and the careless, but the wide scale introduction of power tools during the second half of the 20th century has greatly increased the number of mishaps.

Some of the safety rules which appeared on previous pages are worth repeating here. Keep shears, knives and secateurs closed when not in use. Keep children well away when using power tools. Stand hoes and rakes upright — do not leave them laying about. When not in use store all tools safely in a shed or garage — hanging them on the wall is the best way to avoid problems.

Buy good quality equipment and replace when the useful life of a tool is over. Many accidents occur every year resulting from metal splinters or rusty wheelbarrows, mowers etc.

Finally, do read the manufacturer's instructions before you start to use a new power tool, and do follow what the booklet says.

LAWN MOWERS

A lawn mower is absolutely essential if you have an area of grass, but it is also gardener enemy No.1 in the list of tools and equipment. The 7000 accidents noted on page 50 are nearly all avoidable — just follow the rules below.

Before you begin

Choose a safe model if you are buying a new one. Make sure that it has been approved by an official body such as the British Standards Institute. Make sure that plastic and not metal blades have been fitted if you are buying a rotary or hover mower — these blades won't cut through a cable or the toe of your shoe. Read the instructions carefully. If you already have a rotary mower, replace metal blades with plastic ones.

Put on the right clothes — wear slacks and boots, Wellingtons or stout flat-heeled shoes. Take care when moving the mower on to the lawn — many sprained backs and slipped discs occur annually due to heavy mowers being lifted up stairs or allowed to topple off paths.

Check the mower. Are the plugs firmly in place and is the cable sound? Are the blades properly set? A circuit breaker should be fitted if the mower is an electric one — see page 56 for details.

Walk over the lawn. Remove stones and other debris. You are now ready to begin .... but not if it is raining and you have an electric mower.

Mowing

Drape the cable of an electric mower over your shoulder. Move in a forward direction away from you — never swing from side to side. Cut across slopes — not up and down. Keep children and pets well away. A power mower may suddenly stop, and that spells trouble if you are not careful. The simple drill is to remove the plug of an electric mower or disconnect the sparkplug lead of a petrol one *before* touching the motor or blades. Now you can free clogged grass etc, but do keep your fingers away from the cutting edges. Finally, remember never to leave a power mower unattended when it is on the lawn — a quarter of all lawn mower accidents occur with machines which are not in use.

After you have finished

Clear away all mud, cut grass etc while it is still easy to remove. When putting the mower away in a garage turn the machine away from the line of traffic.

ROTARY CULTIVATORS

Cultivators are not a major source of accidents, but most of them are powerful machines which should be treated with respect. As with all power tools, buy a reputable brand and study the instructions carefully before you start. Put on a stout pair of boots or Wellingtons with reinforced toe-caps and you are ready to start, once you have made sure that no bricks or pieces of rubble are laying on the ground which is to be cultivated.

Don't try to dig too deeply in heavy earth and do let the machine and not your muscle power do the work.

HEDGE TRIMMERS

An electric hedge trimmer is a boon for a person with a large garden — gone are the hours of snipping away with shears. The fast-moving blades make short work of clipping an extensive hedge, but these fast-moving blades can't distinguish between twigs and fingers. The result is that the number of accidents with this tool is frighteningly high.

Before you begin make sure that the plug is in place and that the foliage is not wet — never work in the rain. Put on goggles, gloves and loop the cable over your shoulder. You are now ready to start. The golden rule is that both hands must be firmly on the machine and both feet firmly on a sound base when the hedge trimmer is on. Keep children and pets well away, and stop the machine each time you step forward.

KNIVES & SICKLES

It is a pleasure to watch a skilled gardener using a knife — pruning, grafting, dead-heading and so on. You should not try to copy the technique — in the hands of the inexperienced a knife is a dangerous weapon. Carry a folding pocket knife for cutting twine etc, but use a pair of secateurs for cutting stems. Never leave an open knife laying about — an all-too-common cause of accidents. Scythes, sickles and grass hooks still cause about 1000 mishaps requiring hospital attention every year, even though their use is no longer necessary. An electrically-driven nylon-cord strimmer will trim long grass much more quickly, safely and easily.

CHAINSAWS

The recommendation here is simple — do not use one unless you have been trained. Your local supplier or horticultural college should have details of courses. They will tell you to wear goggles, to hold the saw with both hands at all times, to keep both feet firmly on the ground and so on. But even a properly maintained machine can be unpredictable and dangerous, and many hired machines are not up to standard. Hit a nail or knot with a chainsaw and the blade can hurtle towards you. In untrained hands a chainsaw can be a lethal instrument.

WHEELBARROWS

A surprising inclusion in this section on items of equipment which cause problems, but the humble wheelbarrow is an all-too-frequent cause of back strain. This is nearly always associated with carrying too heavy a load — always consider making two trips instead of one. Unfortunately it is not always possible or practical to divide up the load, and here you have to pay special attention to two points. Firstly you should raise the wheelbarrow legs off the ground as if you were lifting a heavy object — see page 53. Back straight, bend your knees and then straighten your legs. Next, keep the load level and keep away from the edge of the path. Tripping over is a common cause of torn ligaments and strained muscles.

CHAIRS

It is surprising at first glance that furniture should rank so high in the accident list, but then we remember the time we trapped a finger when putting up or closing a deckchair. The old fashioned wooden type has long been something of a menace until the art of opening and folding is mastered. Modern metal chairs, sunbeds, tables etc are usually (but not always) easier to put up, but the same safety rules apply. Keep your fingers well away from the edges and joints when opening or closing. Make sure that both the frame and covering are in sound condition and check that the stays are properly in place before use. Now sit down and relax.

HIRING TOOLS

There are times when we need to use a piece of equipment for a short time but where the high cost rules out purchase. Examples include concrete mixers, hedge trimmers, cultivators and large lawn spreaders. To answer this problem the tool hire industry has grown rapidly in the past few years, and in the main provides a useful service.

Powerful cutting tools are a special case. Unlike a new or carefully maintained machine the hire model will have been used by all sorts of people, and surveys reveal problems. In many instances hire machines such as chainsaws and hedge trimmers have been found to be defective, either electrically or mechanically. When hiring, check the following points. The supplier should be a reputable one and the tool should be clean and sound. Check that the wiring is secure. Try to arrange a demonstration — a complete set of printed instructions is essential. Buy or hire the necessary protective clothing.

Being People Friendly with
Other Danger Spots

ELECTRICITY

Electricity has a vital part to play in the garden these days and you have got to learn to live with it. Outdoor electricity has special rules and you won't learn these from your experience with fitting plugs on table lamps. Do read through the following list — the incidence of fatal electrocutions in the home and garden has increased rapidly in the past few years.

● Look for the BEAB label or BSI kitemark when buying equipment

● Fit a circuit breaker — see the next column

● Always check the lead and plug before use. Make sure that there are no loose connections, frayed wires, missing insulation etc. Make sure you know how to wire a three-pin plug correctly — badly wired plugs cause many accidents every year

● Leads and connectors should be outdoor quality and not designed solely for indoor use. Take care with extension leads — special weatherproof connectors must be used and these should be joined before plugging into the mains. Never join wires together with insulation tape

● Wear rubber- or plastic-soled shoes. Do not use an electrical appliance in the rain

● Make sure the cable is out of the way before you start. With an electric lawn mower, hedge trimmer etc place the cable over your shoulder and work away from it

● Always switch off and unplug if you have to do any cleaning, adjusting, inspecting or stopping for a tea break. Playing with the switch of a power tool has a fascination (sometimes a fatal fascination) for children

● Never pick up the wires before unplugging if you are unfortunate enough to cut through the cable. Obvious, of course, but a cause of numerous deaths every year

● If the job is complex (e.g wiring a greenhouse) or the problem is beyond you (e.g a smell of burnt rubber in the motor), consult an electrician

Circuit Breakers

The purpose of a circuit breaker (also called a power breaker) is to cut off the current if the circuit is broken by the cable being cut or by the equipment becoming live because of a loose connection.

Miniature circuit breakers (MCBs) and plug fuses require some current to flow through before they blow or cut out. The type of circuit breaker you want when working with garden electricity is a **Residual Current Device** (RCD) as this cuts off in three hundredths of a second, which is quick enough to save your life if something goes wrong.

Many types of RCD are available. The simplest is wired like and looks like an ordinary plug — it will cost you about £20. Or you can buy an RCD socket or a portable socket adaptor. Of course only the equipment working on the protected cable is rendered safe. You can have a whole-house RCD unit installed by an electrician but do remember that a fault anywhere in the circuit will cut off all the power.

CHEMICALS

You are almost certain to have chemicals in your shed or garage. Even if you only use natural or organic remedies such as the Bio Friendly range, there are still going to be containers of paints, preservatives, solvents, adhesives etc. Keep them all properly closed. Do not keep packages if the labels are no longer readable and never decant liquid chemicals into unlabelled bottles. Read page 41 for the rules concerning the safe handling of plant protection products.

LADDERS

Using a ladder calls for safety measures — do keep children well away. Place the feet so that the distance from the wall is about a quarter of the height of the top from the ground. Make sure it is firm and straight before you start to climb — place the feet on a large board if the ground is soft. Get someone to hold the sides or place a heavy sack or other large weight against the feet of the ladder. The top must be secure — if in doubt lash it to the tree, window, wall etc. Finally, don't stretch out sideways — move the ladder instead.

HARMFUL PLANTS

Plants not for eating

Scores of garden plants can cause stomach upsets and other undesirable effects when the berries, seeds or other parts are swallowed. Nearly 2000 children go to hospital each year for observation and occasionally for treatment, and so the danger must be taken seriously. But don't panic — fatalities are very rare. Seek medical advice promptly if any part of a plant listed below has been eaten — take along the plant if you can and a sample of vomit if the patient has been sick.

Box (leaves)
Bryony (any part)
Cherry laurel (berries)
Cotoneaster (berries)
Daphne (any part)
Datura (seeds)
Deadly nightshade (any part)

Dieffenbachia (stems)
Foxglove (berries & leaves)
Hellebore (any part)
Holly (berries)
Ivy (berries)
Juniper (berries)
Laburnum (pods)

Lords & ladies (berries)
Mistletoe (berries)
Privet (berries & leaves)
Spindle (berries & leaves)
Sweet pea (berries)
Winter cherry (berries)
Yew (berries)

Taxus baccata (Yew)

Laburnum anagyroides (Laburnum)

Daphne mezereum (Daphne)

Euonymus europaeus (Spindle)

Ligustrum vulgare (Privet)

Plants not for touching

Much less has been written about plant allergies than plant poisoning, but they are much more common and are less easy to avoid. About one in every 5 gardeners is affected at some time. It is wise to wear gloves when handling any of the plants below if you have suffered from a rash, itching or swollen patches on the skin after gardening. Do be especially careful with the plants which cause hypersensitivity to sunlight (marked * below). The sap in the leaves can induce sunburn without prolonged exposure to sunlight.

Bamboo (stems & leaves)
Borage (leaves)
Bugloss (leaves)
Bulbs (sap)
*Carrot (leaves)
*Celery (leaves)
Chrysanthemum (stems & leaves)

Cucumber (stems & leaves)
Daphne (leaves)
Geranium (leaves)
Hellebore (sap)
Marrow (stems & leaves)
Nettle (stems & leaves)
*Parsnip (leaves)

Poinsettia (sap)
Primula (leaves)
Radish (leaves)
Rhus (leaves)
*Rue (leaves & sap)
Strawberry (leaves)
Tomato (leaves)

* Plants which cause hypersensitivity to sunlight

Primula obconica (Poison Primrose)

Chrysanthemum hybrid (Chrysanthemum)

Rhus typhina (Sumach)

Pelargonium hortorum (Geranium)

Raphanus sativus (Radish)

BONFIRES

Bonfires are distinctly not Bio Friendly. Neighbours are annoyed and valuable organic matter is often needlessly destroyed. Compost or dump rubbish whenever you can rather than burn it. The problem is that bonfires are more dangerous than you realise. Of course there is a risk of a fire getting out of control, and breathing smoke is obviously unpleasant for people with asthma or bronchitis.

But there are hidden dangers. Burning foam, old cushions or ceiling tiles can release lethal vapours, and burning green material releases smoke which contains 350 times more cancer-causing chemical than cigarette smoke. Burning preserved timber may release dioxins.

If you *must* have a bonfire then follow the rules. Site it well away from buildings, trees, fences etc and choose a still day. If possible use an incinerator as shown above. Never use paraffin or petrol to start the fire or to liven up a dying one. Burn dry material so that there are flames rather than smoke. It is an offence (maximum fine £2000) to allow smoke to drift across a public road. Keep a bucket of water close by — keep children and pets far away. Never leave a fire unattended and avoid breathing in the smoke.

BARBECUES

The boom in cooking outdoors was one of the remarkable features of the garden scene in the 1980s. Barbecues sold by the million, and accidents were inevitable as people got used to the new and potentially dangerous techniques involved.

Start early. Choose a level site well away from overhanging branches, fences and buildings. Use firelighters or charcoal soaked in a recommended barbecue fuel — never use paraffin, petrol, methylated spirits etc. Never pour fuel on the charcoal once it has been lit. Avoid wearing loose clothing (ties, scarves etc) and keep children well away. Finally, use long-handled utensils and remember that sausages and chicken must be cooked all the way through before serving.

SHEDS

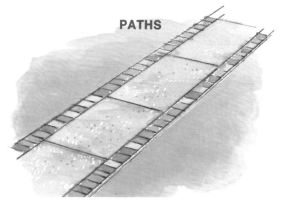

Keep things neat and tidy in the garden shed or the storage part of the garage. This is for safety's sake and also to avoid the frustration of searching for lost items. Hang tools on the walls, close containers and store on shelves, throw away waste material and clean tools, equipment and sprayers immediately after use.

Hazards here are usually quite small, but they increase alarmingly when there are young children in the household — the risk is even greater when the children are visitors and therefore find the garden shed clutter novel and exciting. Make sure that all chemicals are stored or locked carefully away, all cutting tools are safely closed or stowed away and all nails, glass, wire etc are out of harm's way.

PRUNING

Pruning of reasonably-sized trees and shrubs is a straightforward job for the average gardener, but think carefully before undertaking major tree surgery. Removing large branches which are more than head high is a skilled job — injury to person or property can easily occur.

PATHS

The main site of accidents is on paths and driveways — you must therefore pay attention to this area of the garden. Keep all paved areas in good repair — level uneven stones and secure loose slabs. When laying a new path choose a paving material which has a rough surface. It is especially important to make sure that steps are firm and level.

The next job is to keep the surface clear. Remove toys, boxes etc which can pose a hazard for the elderly visitor, absent-minded adult or running child. Sweep away leaves and de-ice in winter. A vital job is to remove slippery algae from the surface — use Garden Jack Path & Patio Cleaner.

CHAPTER 7
Animal Friendly —
CARING FOR
THE CREATURES

No matter how small your garden may be, you will still have to share it with animals. In a tiny urban plot you may be denied the pleasure of watching squirrels scampering over the lawn or hedgehogs ambling along the path, but you will still have birds in the morning and butterflies in the afternoon.

Once gardeners just accepted that the land had to be shared with these 'outsiders'. Nowadays there is a new awareness of the environment, and so there are now millions of people who wish to encourage an increased number of animals to visit or dwell in their gardens.

Much (perhaps too much) has been written about the way wildlife can earn its keep by reducing pest attacks. Animals should be regarded as an ornamental feature of the garden — the sight of frogs and the song of birds should be enjoyed for their own sake. The ability of

wildlife to keep pests under control or of worms to cultivate the soil is rather more limited than some organic devotees would suggest. Still, the pest consumption figures for some garden visitors are indeed impressive. A hedgehog can consume up to 500 slugs in a single night and a family of young tits devour 500 caterpillars a day. Swallows are even more effective — a family in spring may consume up to 8000 insects whilst the young are being reared. This does not mean insects from the garden — the problem is that birds generally forage in the countryside rather than the garden where dangers abound.

There are pets as well as wildlife to consider and here the position is rather different. Virtually nobody wants to attract pets from outside on to the lawn or the flower beds, but we must ensure that the garden is safe both for our own pets and those which unfortunately stray in from outside.

FIVE ANIMAL FRIENDLY FEATURES
FOR THE GARDEN

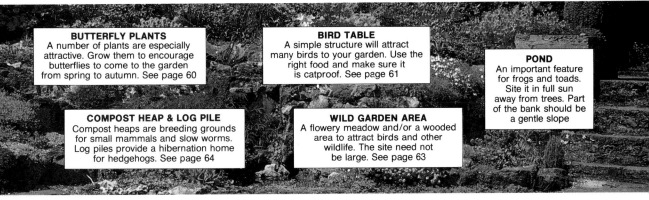

BUTTERFLY PLANTS
A number of plants are especially attractive. Grow them to encourage butterflies to come to the garden from spring to autumn. See page 60

BIRD TABLE
A simple structure will attract many birds to your garden. Use the right food and make sure it is catproof. See page 61

POND
An important feature for frogs and toads. Site it in full sun away from trees. Part of the bank should be a gentle slope

COMPOST HEAP & LOG PILE
Compost heaps are breeding grounds for small mammals and slow worms. Log piles provide a hibernation home for hedgehogs. See page 64

WILD GARDEN AREA
A flowery meadow and/or a wooded area to attract birds and other wildlife. The site need not be large. See page 63

Pets

● Keep the garden free from litter which can be dangerous. Included here are open tin cans, broken glass and patches of spilt oil.

● Ponds are not usually a problem, but kittens and even adult cats sometimes drown. You can avoid a problem by making sure that there is an area of the bank which slopes gently so that an escape route is provided.

● Glass is always a problem, especially if your pet has not got used to its presence. Put some form of marking on the lower panes of a newly-erected greenhouse.

● Tethering a puppy to prevent it from straying or causing damage is certainly not a good idea. Frustration is certain — strangulation is a possibility.

● The danger to cats and dogs from eating sprayed plants is minimal, but you must always follow pesticide instructions on the box or bottle and you must never use a professional product which has no recommendations for garden use. A general rule is to keep pets off the lawn or paths which have been treated with a weedkiller until the area is dry.

● Two products pose special problems — slug killers and mouse poisons. The main risk involves dogs eating the contents of packages — remember that a cereal bait is present which may be regarded as food by your pet. Always close containers and store in a safe place. If you use slug pellets spread them *very* thinly with no two pellets touching. Modern mouse killers such as Racumin are much safer than old-fashioned ones, but it is still a good idea to cover the material so that a mouse but not a dog's head can enter the enclosed baited area.

Wildlife

Attracting Butterflies

There are about 70 species of butterfly classed as British, although some travel here for their summer vacation. Some once-common types have become rarities and nobody really knows why. The environment has of course changed, and hedge removal, pesticides and modern farming have all been blamed. One fact is certain — butterflies are sun-lovers and Britain is close to the northern edge of their ability to survive. This means that the major controlling factor is summer weather — cold and damp conditions will mean that few will visit your garden, no matter how attractive you make it.

Plants which attract butterflies

Butterflies are attracted by the nectar of flowers — blue and purple petals seem to be especially attractive. Plant or sow your butterfly flowers in a sunny spot and make sure you include both spring- and summer-flowering ones. Several seed houses offer 'butterfly mixtures'. Make sure that small plants are grown in clumps and not singly — a mass of flowers is required. One final point — butterflies will visit but not breed in your garden.

Alyssum saxatile
Annual Chrysanthemum
Aubretia
Bedding Dahlia
Buddleia
Candytuft
Forget-me-not
Grape Hyacinth
Hebe
Helichrysum
Heliotrope
Honesty
Ice Plant
Lavender
Michaelmas Daisy
Pot Marigold
Red Valerian
Scabious
Sweet William

Red Admiral
Brimstone
Cabbage White
Small Copper
Comma
Common Blue
Small Tortoiseshell
Holly Blue
Orange Tip
Wall Brown
Painted Lady
Peacock

Attracting Other Wildlife

Thousands of different wildlife species live in or visit your garden — nearly all are lowly creatures such as insects but there will be a number of higher animals. Deer are the largest. Birds, butterflies, hedgehogs and squirrels are the ones considered most appealing — moles and rats share the doubtful honour of being the least desirable. Some, but not all, of the friendly creatures can be encouraged to visit your plot and a relatively small number can be induced to breed there. This latter group includes tits, nuthatches, swallows, frogs, toads, newts, hedgehogs and bats.

HEDGEHOGS are a welcome sight, but you will rarely see them during the day and not at all during the hibernation period in winter. They eat caterpillars and slugs, but they also eat worms and ground beetles. Feed them with cat food rather than milk and leave a pile of cut logs and a heap of leaves in which they can nest.

INSECTS abound in your garden and nearly all of them are harmless. A few are positively friendly as they prey on plant pests. The above-ground pest eaters include ladybirds, lacewings, hoverflies and parasitic wasps. The underground insects which live on soil pests include centipedes and ground beetles. Don't kill them when digging — the general rule is never harm any insect which moves away quickly when you are turning over the soil.

FROGS & TOADS eat the good and the bad — worms and beetles as well as caterpillars, slugs and woodlice. All you need to provide is a pond with an overgrown area nearby in which they can hide from birds during the day and in which they can hibernate during winter. The pond should have an abundance of plant life and should be sloping — a narrow shelf for spawning and a deeper area which will not freeze in winter.

SLOW WORMS are really legless lizards, growing to about 1 ft in length. They are distinctly snake-like but quite harmless to humans. Slugs are their favourite food so don't harm them if they appear when removing compost from the heap or bin. This is their favourite haunt — a log pile (see page 64) makes a suitable alternative home.

Attracting Garden Birds

Winter is a time of food shortage for birds, and many types lose their natural shyness. Set out the tit-bits in the morning and you must supply food regularly once you start. The birds will come to rely on you and can die if the supply is suddenly cut off. Clear away uneaten scraps before adding more food and provide a supply of water. The feeding season extends from October to April. During spring and summer the birds should hunt for their own food — your well-meaning provisions may be quite unsuitable for rearing young chicks.

Plants which attract birds

The plants listed below bear berries, seeds, insects etc which are used as food by birds. There are preferences — robins find the berries of the Spindle tree irresistible whereas bullfinches prefer the seeds of Honesty and Forget-me-not. Leave seed heads on herbaceous border plants. Some shrubs are favoured for roosting and nesting rather than as a source of food — examples include Privet, Conifers, Virginia Creeper and Wisteria.

Alder	Crab Apple	Holly	Snowberry
Barberry	Elder	Honesty	Species Roses
Beech	Firethorn	Honeysuckle	Spindle
Birch	Forget-me-not	Ivy	Sunflower
Bramble	Globe Thistle	Michaelmas Daisy	Viburnum
Cornflower	Golden Rod	Mountain Ash	Willow
Cotoneaster	Hawthorn	Oak	Yarrow

Roof to keep out rain and fallen leaves

Table should be about 5 ft high and at least 6 ft from the nearest branch or wall

Spread out food so that a number of birds can feed at the same time

Provide bacon, fat, suet, proprietary wild bird food, cereals, nuts, dried fruit, cheese and wholemeal bread crumbs

Avoid salted peanuts, desiccated coconut, pieces of white bread, uncooked meat and spicy food

Low wall to prevent spillage

Gap for drainage

Plastic mesh bag or wire tube filled with peanuts, cheese, fat etc

Upturned biscuit tin to deter mice

Bird bath

Birds require water for drinking and bathing, especially in a dry summer and a cold winter. Do not fill too deeply — change frequently.

Common bird table visitors

Blackbird	Goldcrest	Starling
Collared Dove	Nuthatch	Thrush
Dunnock	Robin	Tits
Finches	Sparrow	Wood Pigeon

Thrushes, robins and dunnocks prefer to feed at ground level. Spread out food on the lawn so that many birds can feed at the same time. Always remove food before nightfall

Plastic drainpipe to deter cats and squirrels

CHAPTER 8
Environment Friendly —
KEEPING IT GREEN

Your garden can have only a small effect for either good or ill upon the environment as a whole. All the gardens put together cover about 1½ per cent of the total land area of the U.K. This represents an area which is only a little larger than the King Ranch in Texas and much smaller than the Barley fields of Britain.

It is nevertheless important to garden with the environment in mind and it is possible to help in a limited way. An area can be provided to grow some of the wildflowers which are beginning to disappear from the countryside. A home can be provided for some types of wildlife — the garden pond has become a very important factor in the survival of frogs, newts and toads.

If we cannot help very much then we must make sure that we don't harm the environment. The zone which must concern us most is the immediate area around the house — our neighbourhood. A neglected weed-ridden plot is certainly not a contribution to a better environment — it harms your neighbour. The vigorous weeds which will grow there do not need any help from you for their survival. It is certainly not a 'wild area' in the Bio Friendly meaning of the phrase. A garden wild area must be carefully planned and managed, as described on page 63. A smoke-laden or constantly noisy garden will not disturb the ecology of the nation but it will spoil the environment in which your neighbour lives.

PRESERVING HARDWOODS

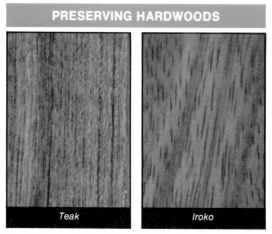

Teak   Iroko

Much of the garden furniture sold today is made of plastic or metal — hard-wearing, easy to maintain and often inexpensive. But for some there is nothing to take the place of hardwood benches, chairs and tables. Teak has long been the favourite type — it is resistant to water, rot and fire. But it is costly, and cheaper items of furniture are made from W African Iroko or red-coloured Meranti from Malaysia.

It is sometimes stated that it is environmentally damaging to buy furniture made from tropical hardwood. Equatorial forests are being felled for this purpose, and this loss of leaf cover is increasing the greenhouse effect which is threatening the earth.

Felling of wild forests is indeed taking place on a large scale in Brazil, but this is for land clearance rather than for commercial timber — it would go on if the wood was sold or not. Less than one tenth of the tropical hardwood used by manufacturers in Britain comes from Brazil — more and more comes from managed forests located elsewhere in the world. Buying products made from this 'managed' wood actually helps the environment. If hardwoods were no longer bought then the managed forests would be of no value. The sites would then be cleared and planted with cash-yielding but environmentally-useless crops.

PRESERVING PEAT

Sphagnum Peat   Sedge Peat

There is concern these days that the peat resources of the world are being steadily depleted by the increase in its removal for horticultural and other purposes. There are still vast bogs in Canada, Russia and Finland which have hardly been touched, but half the lowland fens of Britain have been lost.

Sedge peat is the type dug from English heaths and moors. It is dark and rather heavy — the brown mass is made up of the remains of sedges, rushes and heather. Sphagnum (or moss) peat is quite different. This is the type which is found in Iceland, Canada, Norway, Finland, Ireland and Russia. It consists of the undecayed remains of sphagnum moss — the spongy material is fluffier and more pleasant to handle than sedge peat. Sphagnum peat is also lighter, more acidic and much more absorbent.

The world reserves of sphagnum peat (the base for Bio Friendly Universal Compost) are much higher than those of the sedge type, but it is necessary to use all types of peat sensibly to avoid shortages in the years to come. Don't use peat for overall soil improvement — it is not very efficient and garden compost or manure will do a much better job. Use it only where there are no substitutes of equal merit — in potting composts, seed composts and planting mixtures.

THE WILD AREA

More and more people who have the ground to spare are devoting a patch of their garden to growing plants which are native to or naturalised in this country and which give the area a wild or natural look. There is the added benefit that birds, butterflies and other creatures may be provided with food or a home. Such a garden feature is often called a 'wild area', but this is a misleading name in the case of a garden meadow. It certainly cannot be left unattended to look after itself — it usually requires quite careful management. Failure to do so often results in aggressive plants fairly quickly swamping the delicate ones — the ones you are probably trying to encourage and protect.

The Garden Meadow

A garden meadow is a grassy area into which native plants are introduced and allowed to flower. Cutting takes place once the flowering season is over.

If the chosen area is clothed with fine grass you can raise wildflowers from seed in pots and then plant them out with a small trowel or bulb planter in spring or autumn. Where coarse grasses such as Rye grass predominate then it is better to start from scratch. Strip off the turf and sow one of the grass/wildflower mixtures which are offered by several seedsmen. Alternatively you can sow a fine grass seed mixture at the low rate and when established plant with wildflowers as described above.

Do not use a fertilizer before creating or when maintaining a garden meadow. Dig out coarse and aggressive weeds such as docks and thistles when they appear.

When cutting time arrives (see below) it is essential to rake off and remove the clippings within a day or two. Use a strimmer and cut the grass about 3 in. high.

Spring meadow
Spring-flowering plants:
Bugle
Cowslip
Daisy
Lady's Smock
Snake's Head Fritillary
Star of Bethlehem
Wild Daffodil
Yellow Rattle

Cut from July until the grass stops growing in late autumn

Summer meadow
Summer-flowering plants:
Crane's-bill
Kidney Vetch
Knapweed
Lady's Bedstraw
Ox-eye Daisy
Ragged Robin
White Campion
Yarrow

Cut in April/May. Start again in late September and continue until grass stops growing in late autumn

The Garden Thicket

A garden thicket is a woody area which is planted primarily with native species and is arranged in several layers. First of all there are the trees if you have room, below which are the shrubs and then the wildflowers. At the base is the litter — a layer of dead leaves, twigs etc. Most gardeners do not have room for full grown trees and shrubs, so it is quite usual to trim the larger specimens. In this way a mixed hedge is produced.

The garden thicket is a haven for wildlife. Hedgehogs and mice nest in the surface litter. Birds, bees and butterflies gather around the flowers, seeds and berries. Leaves serve as food and nesting material for animal types which shun the 'foreign' fare offered by garden plants.

Try not to disturb the garden thicket — cleaning it up will frighten away some of the wildlife. However, some work is necessary for the first couple of years. Water in dry weather during the first year after planting and prune back the shoots during the first winter so that bushy growth will be encouraged. Mulch with bark and old leaves for 2 or 3 years.

Trees & Shrubs
Alder
Birch
Blackthorn
Dog Rose
Dogwood
Elder
Guelder Rose
Hawthorn
Hazel
Holly
Maple
Rowan

Climbers and Wildflowers
Bluebell
Crane's-bill
Foxglove
Hart's-tongue Fern
Honeysuckle
Ivy
Lily of the Valley
Old Man's Beard
Primrose
Snowdrop
Solomon's Seal
Violet
White Campion

PRESERVING THE OZONE LAYER

Much has been written about the danger of CFC propellants which were widely used until recently in aerosols. These chemicals have been linked to the damage which is occurring to the ozone layer around the earth, and so the propellants now used in garden aerosols are hydrocarbons and not CFCs.

This has solved one problem and caused another. The new propellant makes the aerosol more susceptible to heat than when CFC was used. It is now more important than ever to store canisters in a cool place, to avoid spraying near a naked flame and to keep away from children. Make sure that you spray at arm's length and that you hold the canister no closer to the plants than the label recommends.

MOWER FUEL

Two star petrol has gone and unleaded petrol has arrived. You will of course want to use the unleaded grade — the rule is that new mowers can run on unleaded petrol but you will have to have the engine cleaned before changing over if the mower has been used with leaded petrol for a season or more. Some mowers will run on four star petrol and others won't — get in touch with the service department of the manufacturer for advice.

WASTE DISPOSAL

Gardens create an astonishing amount of waste material. Turn grass mowings, soft prunings, non-flowering weeds and vegetable plant remains into compost — see page 8 for instructions. Bag up woody material, diseased plants, thick vegetable stalks etc and dispose of safely. This calls for taking it to a public dump or getting in touch with the local waste disposal authority who will get rid of it at a small charge. If you do intend to have a fire read the 'Bonfires' section on page 58 and follow the instructions carefully. Check that there are no bye-laws which forbid the burning of garden rubbish.

Dispose of waste pesticide solutions by spraying on plants (if permitted on the label), bare ground or a gravel path — keep well away from ponds and watercourses. Don't pour liquid down the drain. Empty pesticide packs should be tightly secured, wrapped in several sheets of newspaper and put in the dustbin.

PRESERVING PLANTS IN THE WILD

However well-meaning your intentions it is quite wrong to dig up plants from their natural habitat in order to grow them in your own garden. You may wish to save them from extinction, but remember that the plants are succeeding in their own special environment and will probably find conditions in your garden quite unacceptable. Primroses might succeed anywhere, but ferns, alpines, orchids etc certainly will not. Then there is the legal issue — you can collect seeds but it is against the law to remove plants without permission.

It is also necessary to avoid buying bulbs and plants which have been uprooted from their natural habitat and shipped to Britain for sale. Of course you cannot always tell, but some suppliers do include a note on the labels that their bulbs are raised on a nursery and are not dug up from the wild.

THE LOG PILE

A log pile will provide an excellent home for a variety of small and not-so-small creatures. Though not particularly unsightly it is best constructed in an out-of-sight spot. Behind the garden shed or next to the compost heap is ideal. Lay down a pile of sawn logs with a heap of leaves nearby, or make a small raised bed with logs, filling it and some (not all) of the crevices with peat-enriched soil. Plant with woodland types such as Primrose, Lily of the Valley, Bluebell and Solomon's Seal. Animals and plants which may take up residence include hedgehogs, frogs, toads, newts, black beetles, snails and toadstools.

GOOD NEIGHBOURS

A householder who enjoys a regular Sunday afternoon nap and a neighbour who always chooses that time to cut the lawn are set on a collision course. So are the bonfire builder and the regular user of an outdoor washing line. The list of local pollutants (noise, smell, smoke etc) is unfortunately a long one — try not to be a cause of harming the local environment.

If you do then your neighbour's first step will be to approach the local council. They will stop you if you are breaking a bye-law. Where that doesn't apply a writ can be issued if the annoyance you are causing is both regular and prolonged. Court cases are costly and the outcome is always unpredictable. It is so much better if you can listen reasonably to the initial complaint and do something about it if you can. In addition inform your neighbour if you are going to create a temporary disturbance such as using a noisy power tool or erecting a fence.